SCOUNDRELS of DEFERRAL

Poems to Redeem Reflection

SCOUNDRELS of DEFERRAL

Poems to Redeem Reflection

Toyin Falola and Vivek Bahl

CAROLINA ACADEMIC PRESS
Durham, North Carolina

ISBN 10: 1-59460-338-3
ISBN 13: 978-1-59460-338-9
LCCN: 2006933852

Carolina Academic Press
700 Kent St.
Durham, NC 27701
Telephone (919) 489-7486
Fax (919) 493-5668
www.cap-press.com

Printed in the United States of America

Preparation and Cover
Saverance Publishing Services
Brooklyn, NY

For Leku

through whom we discover

what the eyes cannot see

For Pasitor

through whom we discover

what the ears cannot hear

Table of Contents

PART B / Reflections of Agonies ◆◆

PART C / *Transcending Agonies* ⸻◇◇⸻

Preface

This collection of poems was written as an exploration of the possibilities of movement in the midst of professional, communal and familial obligations. Perhaps there is no right or wrong place to be in the world or in life, only what we are able to do with the locations in which we find ourselves. Still, at any given moment, we can also be painfully aware that much remains to be done, that we have not yet found a way to answer the heart's yearnings, whether for purposeful action, social justice, or personal fulfillment. As we know, yearnings can goad one to great action, and they can also produce frustrated paralysis, the legs turned to steel, the body chained to massive pillars. No matter our accomplishments and functionality in many dimensions of our lives, some of the poems interrogate blocks, anxieties, and insecurities. We asked, what have been the obstacles to movement, to persuading the soul to engage in history more intensely? Is it a problem of analysis, of will, of vision, or that the implicit and explicit sparks of hope and faith have been too narrow and unimaginative?

Beyond what may be a universal (or bewildering) set of dilemmas described above, these poems emerge from and seek to re-engage the uneven, uncharted terrain of migrancy, dispersal, and cultural marginality, and the heroic or failed attempts to arrive at voice, authority and forceful identity within treacherous spaces. One of the authors grew up in the United States, as part of what is known as the 1.5 generation of immigrants from India; the other, a Nigerian, migrated in his adulthood, still early in his career. The migrant may routinely face the slings and arrows of misunderstanding, exclusion, competition, mistrust, or vilification. Even the desire to be generous and hospitable can be perceived as manipulative or oppressive, as though power were a zero-sum game. And yet, there is much for migrants to learn, for we are not immune to misreading ourselves, others, and the future. Our duties are to find what is immaterial in the slings and arrows, to learn to maneuver with agility through those that are real, to clear the heart of fear and hatred, to refuse the retreat from desire, to receive the good will of others, to discover spaces of grace, to regenerate collective possibilities, and to work.

So why poetry? Some of the poems are confessional in nature, and we worried about the potential self-indulgence in devoting so much time and effort towards what might be perceived as mere personal reflection. And yet, if the dilemmas are real, if certain forms of paralysis are unrelenting, then the project of aestheticizing struggle, giving some shape to the chaos of yearning, and paying obeisance to the sacred capacity for creativity may be a worthy gamble.

While many must surely identify with the often elusive, sometimes catastrophic and largely unintended power of deferral and delay, we hope that our reflections and engagements here have moved beyond individual quandary. Deferrals can be private – significant or inconsequential – and they can also be public and momentous. Given our social and political commitments, this is a book that attempts to ground and sustain individual action, intention and labor on behalf of community and collective needs. Alas, the ideal of the collective not only can drown the individual but can, perhaps more damagingly, leave the individual with a sense of uselessness or the impossibility of serious, commensurate contribution. The energies for these poems emerge from a conviction that migrations and dislocations can be exciting and hopeful as well as heartrending and diminishing, but that they always offer choice. These poems seek to refuse paralysis in defiance of any empirical evidence that may be taken from an individual life. Indeed the poems also reveal the transformations, if not resolution, of contradictions; the joys of finding connection; and the suturing together of new traditions and communities, even from frayed and ruptured fabrics. In a time of expanding empire, many poems register outrage and undertake the labor of imagining our struggles for dignity and justice.

Some readers, of course, may not relate to the impasses described here and the struggles we have undertaken to overcome them, nor to the celebration, laughter and joy that the poems also discern and bespeak. Your pains and strategies of hope may be different. But whether or not you find echoes of your own experiences here, know that the poems seek to be an audience for you as well.

Toyin Falola and Vivek Bahl
Austin-Seattle, Fall 2005

It is no small wonder that a volume of writing taking on the dreaded theme of deferral would ever be completed. Anyone who is even fleetingly familiar with the output of one of the authors will quickly recognize the supreme improbability of his inclusion as one of "the scoundrels of deferral"! In truth, what began as an individual effort to explore and transcend the burdens, the traumas, the pleasures, the truths, the losses, the gains, the vagaries, and the lessons of deferral could never have come to fruition without that pluralization. And so the poems are also born of affection. Affection as magic, as elixir, as antidote incubated in the uneven and rich margins thrown together through the unpredictable vectors of diaspora and dislocation. What greater gift of friendship can there be than to lend one's creative talents to another's triumph, and to drag poetry and light from a reluctant source?

Isola, the scion of Agbo

He who devours all of life and grins

Who hungers for the good and worthy

Who feasts upon sorrows and pain

Who tears apart treachery with his teeth

Isola, find the hidden food of history

Spread the banquet of justice and joy

Isola devours hunger and still can eat some more.

Isola, conquer the earth

Carve the tree of life with your art

Lift the people to let them breathe their strength

Sing to them their laughter

Seduce them with their gifts

Isola, the hijacker of despair

Changing the destination from fear to creativity

The venture capitalist

Investing the overabundance of love and labor.

Isola races ahead of the day

Faster than duty left to gasp for breath

Run faster, racing around the globe

The hare teaching the tortoise to fly

Isola, don't stop to receive thanks

The thunderbolt brings forth the rain

Isola, don't stop to rest

Eyes that close slowly but never stop seeing.

Acknowledgments

We must acknowledge the generosity of our initial readers and critics, a varied cast of students and professors, poets and literary critics, citizens and strangers: Jaeney Hoene, A. B. Assensoh, Tola Mosadomi, Andrew Clarno, Hank Galmish, Rahdi Taylor, Chris Denton, Fariba Ghorbani, Seema Srinath, David Lee Powell, Eric Nelson, Sundeep Dougal, Barbara Harlow, Tola Agbetuyi, Michael Hall, Marcie Sims, Lotus, Andy Anderson, Rosalyn Howard, Omi Osun, Ben Lindfors, Laura Saponara, Joseph Oster, Tyrell Stewart, Jane Boone, Rasheed Na'Allah, James Sidbury, Manolo Callahan, Rebecca Gámez, Jordan Camp, Nadia Raza, Mia Carter, Steven Huff, Page Laws, Haruna Garuba, Rahul Gupta, Anjulie Ganti, Maysaloun Faraj, Mary Hogan Camp, Tejumola Olaniyan, and Marian Barber. The entire membership of the Arizona Bahl-Narla clan was more than eager to celebrate and honor our writing: Prem and Lakshi Bahl along with Aru, Neeru and Akhila Narla.

We cannot name or express adequate thanks to those audiences who listened to a few of the poems on public occasions. We acknowledge all those who offered indispensable critical commentary, praise and, most of all, bounteous enthusiasm, and wanted to see this book in print much earlier than this. What can we now say to those who assisted us, other than that they were warned not to expose themselves to the world as the associates of two unrepentant scoundrels!

In illustrating the book, we fall on the professional expertise of the following excellent photographers: Mohammad Jobaed Adnan, Oscar Belen, Roy Doron, A. Olusegun Fayemi, John Gibler, Stephanie Hynes, Suman Kathuria, Adam Lambert-Gorwyn, Henk Leerssen, Tehilah Leonard, Piotr Lewandowski, Patrick Navin, Gary Oliveira, Devin Theriot-Orr, Mira Pavlakovic, Kevin Rohr, Laura Saponara, Clyde Saverance, Sam Saverance, Kavitha Shivan, Ricky Tolboom, Miguel Ugalde, Leslie Vega, and Madhur Verma. They graciously bestowed their creativity, warmth and universal spirit in order to highlight or enhance the various thematic strands in the poems. We thank them for adding immeasurably to the richness of this book.

PART A

Agonies of Reflections

Reverse Psychology

Don't rush to read this book, as
Many more are ahead in your queue.
You never read those others, and
What harm ever came from that?
How one laughs at those who are
Fervent and grave, yet again
Having found something new.
Drunk with their own conversion,
They're off to spread the wealth.
Yes, such naïveté could endear
If it didn't annoy instead.
Whatever I took from the book,
I'm no fool to edify you.

You'll glance at the book, just as all
The others got the once over.
If it doesn't grab you, my goodness,
That's surely no fault of your own.
Why, even sex and violence
In unskilled hands are made
Dreary and drab and dull.
You're widely read and deeply
Thought; your life could itself
Make a much richer book!

You're not so jaded as not
To concede that the book may yield
A trifle or two, but what's
Truly new in this world?
You'll intend to read this book
One day, of this much I am
Sure. Till then, let your eye
Taste some other delights
Where nicer nutrition may lie.
Let no one disrupt your plans,
Or amend your fixed reading list.

Bookshelves are capacious creatures,
Equalizing and disguising what's
Potent, mediocre, sublime.
True, the books at the bottom
Endure the greatest neglect,
Rescued only when your dinner
Guests, too, are ignored.
My book takes its humble
Place, no concession for being
New. It's survival of the fittest
Or simplest or best dressed;
It competes now with all the rest –
Tough love for the culpable book.

In Search of Shame

Who exiled shame, oh king?
Lament the banishment
Shame was watchful
Shame knew our hearts
The judge and the accused, not far apart.

Shame is a contract
A promise of tomorrow unshackled from yesterday
A humble bow before the august assembly of the All in oneself.
The aforementioned party
Heretofore known as Shame
Agrees to hold harmless
    the thoughtless for his carelessness
    the passionate for her selfishness
    the curious for his naughtiness
    the fervent for her ardor
    the confused for his complexity
    the defiant for her refusals
    the lazy for his wonderment
    the accused for her exuberance
There is no jurisprudence for this breach.

Shame is an invitation
To forgive oneself quickly
Less than a day, rarely more than two
Shame invites forgetting
Erasing dead traces of dead actions
The buoyed spirit racing along new verdant rivulets.

Shame's invitation refused or undelivered
No sustenance of admonishment's food
No sparking of forceful hope
No relief of raucous tumbling
An empty banquet
A grieving silence
The mockery of joy.

Shame's labor lost
The lost magic of the look
The look that can strike fear
The look that can transform
The look that embraces
The look refracted, deflected, murdered.

The solitary refinement of the shameless
Is a frenzied lurching
The quick left arm of defense
The avaricious right hand that snatches
Seeking indulgence without consequence
Catharsis without accountability
The barren land of the free.

No longer guide but taskmaster
No longer judge but executioner
No longer elder but gnarled death
There is no life in this defiance.

I will mount an army
for your triumphant return
I invite you, I invoke you
I have searched for you
Amongst homeless longings
and discarded tears
Find me again
Your strong supple fingers
Repairing my torn ligaments of hope and innocence.

The Prisonhouse of Frozen Wisdom

I pace within the cell of
Poised words of good intention.
But I am resourceful
I plan my escape!
I test each bar
I know their weakness
I feel my strength
I will grasp their worth,
Unmoor them into weapons,
Striding three- and four-fisted
The gentle-fierce man about town.

Look, the determined face fallen,
So soon exhausted by hope,
Traveling without destination to
Reawakened confinement.
No reprieve from the protecting pause,
The unescaped weight of wasted balance.
Let me decorate these prison walls
With poignant portraits of justification.
These chains are holiday garlands
Of brave resignation and dutiful repression.
The sun shines bright
The moon peers in.

Desire deferred is desire denied.
Only if I can be angry
Can I let you be angry.
I am angry
But I am not Anger.
Schemes of Love
Glimmers of Faith
Jostle now
To take the stage.
Anger vanished
But vanquished not.
These walls are permeable,
Conduits the bars.
Well, come again.

My Cross

My body of contradictions
unable to resolve the
confounding of my mind
A heart
heavy with sorrow
The brain
swimming in a skull
loaded with bullets
of ideas.

No matter the riddles
I answer
the paradoxes
I transcend
I am lost in confronting
and solving
cold concepts.
Should I not rather
see and explain
the hills and thickets?

No matter how tenacious
the burden
or significant
the realization
I cannot be born again.

Catharsis

I.
Anger and Disappointment
Desire and Fear
Longing and Sadness
Loss and Mourning
Those moments when the tears flowed
The sudden clarity and connection
Authenticating the feeling self –
I cannot reconstruct those moments.

Self sympathy
Self involvement
Squandering time
Disappointing
Wounding others
or myself
Without much sense
of how to fix anything.

II.
I repressed my pain
I wasn't entitled to my anger
Who would take it seriously,
Acknowledge it?
Inflicting instead a price
for daring to grimace at
the prerogatives of
a bullying power.

I opted for victimhood
to display my suffering
Multiplying victimization
Turning inwards and waiting
Not seeing myself
as claiming the rights of a victim.

The pathos of a confrontation
A history of humiliation
A cultural space and language
within which cries for
Justice and Dignity
might be heard.
Missing for me,

Subject to old and new violence
Punished in shifting
Responsibility for self
Onto others –
A disavowal of agency.

III.
The delicate urgency
Of sympathy with others
Witnessing
Embodying
And yet alone again
Mourning loved ones
Pain
Suffering
Depression
Obligations
The unretreating Real.

Poorly channeled emotions
in the course of an ordinary life
Displacements and Deferrals
Illusions and Delusions
Blindness and Insight
All gushing out
in the breaching of a dam.

IV.
When I relinquished her
I fled
Suffocated by shame
Confounded
Fragmented
Desiring to reform
Desiring to rebel
Losing faith in self and home
Not having known
where to turn
or to whom.

Yearning earnestly
for a way to be ethical
Decent
Loyal –
Ah, what bathos
All this!

Snatches of light
showed me
that I could picture
myself still
as decent, good, legitimate
Rediscovering God just then,
the rushing grace of joining
the streams of everything
Noble and Dignified –
Dead
Living
Unborn.

V.
Simple emotions
Rare moments
when one can access them
Sympathy
for self and others
Entitlement
The right to have care
The claimed right to care for others
Finding without thinking
Breathing deep the spirit
of being loved.

The regular flow of
emotions in a healthier life
Without intention
Without naming.

The Secret Self

My mind tarries
I look to the sky
All its emptiness
Tortured insights
Of a life
Wasted in reflection,
Insights in search of
Another world.
Emotions, energies
Distributed
Without meaning.

Difficult times
Managed recklessly
I pleaded with myself
At least
Undertake
Small activities, daily tasks:
    begin them
    be in the
    finish them
Discover the rhythms of
Completion and satisfaction.

Unconscious
Often conscious
Investments in
Grandiosity and elitism
Narratives and fantasies to
Transcend the mundane.

The grandiose self
Kept an eye on
The resplendent future,
Static and undefined.
Past moments
Glimpsing glory
Fawned over like trophies.

All eyes are on me
Except I pretend
My frozen future
Impacts none.

An idealized future
Serving as a blind spot,
A closing off
Not an enabling hope.

The story is not yet complete.
An unended life
Looking forward
To compensate for
The troubles of the present.

I have produced a secret life
The celebration of the
Sweet pain of desire
Left in a state of
Anticipation
The secret self
Not expressed
Only released.

Bereft

Aggregated minds
Commune of feelings
Disentangled classes
Disaggregated ethnicities
In the laboratory of complexities

Invented nostalgia
Oils the machinery of homelessness
Roaming streets of despair
Searching for the
Hopeful rotunda
Of stars in the making

Disconnection

I am trapped
Doomed to lose
Emotions in disarray
Unraveled relations
Feasts of pain
Heritage in cage
Friendships swim to drown.

The eyes of my sun are lost
The land dries up
Even our tears are not united
Yours rejoice
Mine regret.

Spiritual engineering?
Solitary versus collective?
Emotions of intellectuals,
Or intellectuals of emotions?

Can the caring daring
Labor of politics
Heal my wounds?
I come to attention and salute,
Awaiting the answers again,
and yet again
    intentional collective?
    collective intentional?
    sacrifice of humility?
    humility of sacrifice?
    liberal redemption?
    bourgeois collaboration?
Shine my sun
Open your eyes.

Another Day

Today may be the new day
to wonder again
before today goes.
Perplexity reflexivity
about me and you
as I think of the revolution for us
on a day that
I am not happy.

Happy day,
Where are you?
To create the revolution of a new day
a new hope
I turn in bed, telling myself this:
 put your life on track
 knowledge is not enough
 do deep work
 produce the analysis
 break the patterns.

Telling myself that
I must run away,
not from you,
from me, to ask:
 What would be good to do?
And, yes,
 Can the good achieve the impossible?
I need an answer now:
 the genius to avoid rigor
 to escape pain
If only to transcend the day:
 the unrelenting limitations
 the floundering
 for days moments months.

My answer may lie in vision
As I lay in bed
Thinking, asking:
 What have been the obstacles to doing all that would be good to do?
 How important is it to acknowledge this history?
 What are the preconditions for overcoming the obstacles to doing?
 How can we usher in those preconditions?
Let the task begin
On another day.

Ruined Time

My house of time in ruins
The crumbling walls
The fractured floor
What turmoil and malice
Conspire beneath the surface
To assemble my paralysis?

At first
Casual carelessness
Trifling neglect
Only
A minor error
A mild postponement
Then
Anxiety and avoidance
Paint the walls
The pillars of
Shame and panic
Erected
Encircled with garlands of neglect.

Seeking comfort
Finding forgetting
In the nowness of pleasure.
Overdue tasks
Cast their shadows
And shame's dominion
Destroys duties daily.
What chance has
Today's terror
Against
Yesterday's embarrassment?

I wait too long
Doing the wrong thing first
A fragile foundation
Crushed by temptation
Sacred time
Carved for work
Shattered in distractions
The beams splintered
Under duress.

Public duty becomes
The personal drama
Of betrayal and catastrophe.
The roof of rest and shelter
Decayed to leave me
Naked and condemned
How long must I endure
This suffocating embrace?
The simplest of deferrals
Fueling formidable failures.

Fatigue

My legs are weak
They refuse to run
Or they will not walk
Mind and heart separated
To blind the eyes.

Work grinds to a halt
Consuming fabrications
Interrupting worthy chores.
Urgency becomes the enemy
Killing purpose
Damaging routine.
The body aches with
The overflow of thoughts
Washing away intention.

New promises
Enliven me
Surprise me
To birth knowledge
To trust discipline
To discard desires
Waiting for
The pain to leave.

Ponderous Rest

I am lazy today
I won't work tomorrow
I will sleep all day
The day after
Not to wake for days

I am lazy
Understand me
But I dream
A fantasy of work

Someone must do the work
Of creating meaning
Carrying sorrows
Inventing, expanding
Horizons of possibility and joy
Protecting, strengthening
Hope and dignity

I have no part, no path
All this is too damn much for me.
Do your small part
Not our small part

But, I dream with vision
Major responsibilities
Annoy the casual hobbyist.
My laziness
Is generous and fraternal.
I bequeath not the labor
To hapless individuals

I rest no more
Let the *collective spirit*
Fulfill its duty
By any means necessary.
Accountability must not
Fall through the cracks.
I awake,
Never to sleep again.

Struggles without a Room

I fight with no one
No, the tongue is locked in the mouth
Closed jaws, clenched teeth
Strangers to peace
Soldiers in the battle of living.

My fumbling and chaos
Are below par for the course
If I see some at peace
    working with purpose
    triumphing over alienation
    as Mama's dedication in the kitchen
I remain baffled still.

A new mind
New questions emerge
Seriousness of work
Productive energy
To be found
How to be a warrior at peace?

Peace without tradition?
Arguments without maturity?
An homage for an adversary
For me to claim the path
Define the course
Still, my tears do not end.

I make room for you
As legs make way for thorns
Make no room for me
Remove the mats to lie
The intimacy of troubles
The closeness of leprosy
The trust who closes the door
Leaving no room for me.

Self Dialogue

Sharpened knife, oh
Do not stab me
Wait for the ink to dry
To pour out words.
Deafness of the ears
Not of sight
As the mind strikes back.

Oh, the left holds the knife
The right hand wields
A pen full with ink
Striking the paper in anger.

The anger of ambiguities
Reproduction in column one
Column two marks the revolution
Reform stays in the attic
Awaiting my ladder.

My legs bid commands:
Forget the charts
Take the highway of reproduction
From space to earth
From science to art
Unorthodox, I walk.

There is no peace for the chicken
Until the hawk leaves the sky.
Revolution cannot forget
This bread I must eat
The daily unique
The excellent ordinary
Resonating with the traditional
The bridge to the radical.

Teach but learn
Keep the past but walk
Walk, walk
Look left: politics
Look right: protest
Look back: solidarity
Look front: autonomy

Add to the addictions
For the legs
To acquire wings
Blown high
To the storms of evil.

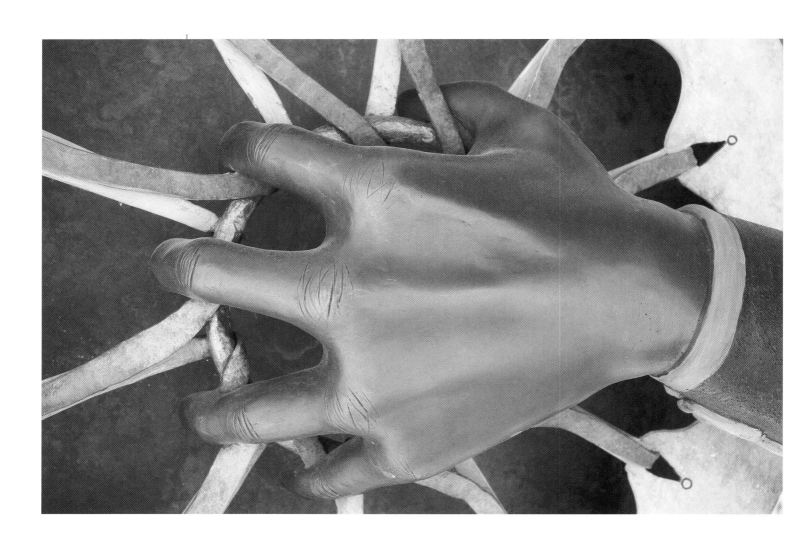

Medusa

Do not see me
To turn my head into stone
I have no Perseus
The invincible to behead

I run
Diseases in front,
Oh! Medusa
Wars everywhere
Poverty
Oh! Medusa
Three-legged dagger
Plucking my eyes and nose

I bleed
In the valley of sadness
Vacated by love
I sing
Sorrowful drums
Trumpets of death
To ears of pain

Come, Medusa
Strike
Turn me into clay
An ugly mold
For Perseus to cry

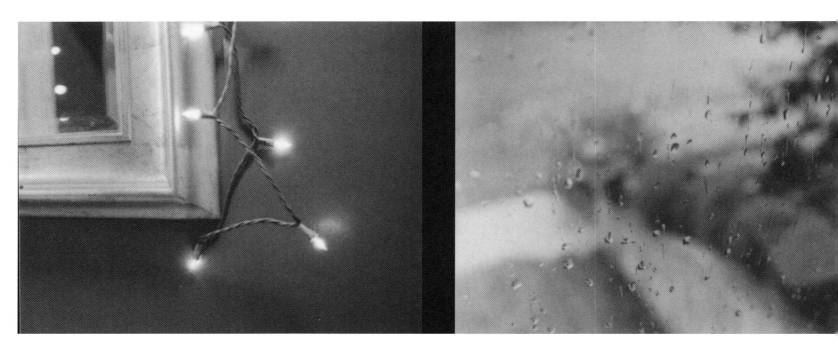

Wizards of the Day

When I see rain
I call it sun
Feeling hot air
I stagger
The sun refuses to rise or set
Fate and hope turn sour
As I review the chapters.

I thought everything rested
On my brilliance
    personal life
    relationships
    all writing
    all play
    sexuality
    even desire itself
Imagine the alienation:
Brilliance as the basis for the social!

My hopes keep changing
I err, yet again
As calamity unfolds.
If not brilliance
Then what?

Offer me solace
Read me as a book –
    sympathetically
I plead for feedback –
    humbly
I yearn for grace –
    silently

Teachers of change
I no longer seek brilliance
Brilliant teachers, let us depart
Brilliant books, I forsake
Teach me values
To engage with tangible horizons
To enflesh politics and ethnicity.

I said engagement
Combinations and intersections
Solace, reply
The platter of new horizons
Pursued with the rigor
Of trust and adventure
To land me in another land
Singing new echoes
Of rebirth.

Room 101

A hall soaked in tension
Words launched as blows
To empty stomachs.
Rhythms of pretence
Whispers of fear
A club of scorpions
Sharing profound ideas
About idiocy.

ABD (All But Dissertation)

The demise is soon:
    slim content
    short thesis
    masquerading insights
Save me,
terrible mentors.

I forsake brilliance
I didn't read just
to demonstrate genius.
I seek affection,
a relationship
based not on
the ugly pawnshop
of knowledge.
Give me the luxury of
long acquaintance
with the space
to display my talents,
but never never make them
the engines of connection.

I have a future
espoused as
the battle for references,
brutal relations
as a member of a class
presumably
with a purpose.

I seek the end of brilliance:
Offer me interventions
present advice
take sufficient care
to learn, to remember
the details of my life.

Director,
banish brilliance,
invite friendship.
I will give you
something in return
not a thesis
not a card.
Oh, how could I ever
give anything back?

Intelligentsia of Doom

Splotches of human blood
Accenting carpets on confused floors
Roofs of burnt houses
Sheltering dark minds
Elite self-images
Blind to the unfolding violence
Reproducing diminished cultures
The mimicry of shame
The exaltation of shamelessness
In bed with mendacity
The hymnals of racism
Compiled in lawns of hypocrisy
To harmonize verses of greed.

The Lazy Scholar

Speak on!
The space is empty
Write!
Without evidence
Work!
Without pain
Committee work
Consumes
The lazy scholar
Now a cripple.

Flaws are flavors
As the yard looks green
The patio is shaded
Posing the pregnant
Questions of anarchism.

Enliven the brightness of
Authority Nonsense:
Who can contest
What they say?
How to explain why
We are seduced,
Compelled by
Even a single insight?
The insights of profanity.

Tenured Professor

Without luck
Leaving behind time
Lost connections
Eluded success
Of vain struggles

Where is the promised land
If only to ask
How I made it?
The turning points
    seizing opportunities
    as the hawk mates the hen
Conformists in the danger land

Pungent allure of failure
Informal guilds of mourners
Bugs of depression
    sneaking into my pockets
Pains of sorrow
    grasping collapsing dreams

Sacrifices too many
Blood shed at the altar of insanity
Lucky breaks
In a life devoid of magic

All for You

Have I lost you?
You who bequeathed me silence
for travel without prayer,
a desert soujourn
bereft of oasis.

Where is my destination?
Mapless and unreprieved,
my spirit in tatters;
jagged is the path
to drain my purpose.

Is confusion my legacy?
A victim of compromises
and abandoned faith,
doubts strapped to my body
to wander without honor.

Will I remain exhausted?
Fatigue crafted painstakingly
from animated indecision,
a treasuring past estranged
from its constricted future.

Has hope evaded me?
That dignity may be snatched,
that worldly demand not
trump impassioned vision,
that rest will cherish me at last.

Shall I give up?
My loving promises broken,
loveless taboos desecrated
on the ravaged road
to a decaying triumph.

Why must I be alone?
Purchase a portion of my anguish,
press my faithlessness to your bosom
as you travel to the promised land where
a horizon keeps secrets but does not lie.

Lovelessness

They all left me
One by one
One to a place of no address
The other to a ruthless man
Madness stalks yet another.

We all toil
In the turmoil of recovery
One suffers from headaches
The migraines of guilt
Awaiting my forgiveness.

The other has heartaches
Pounded by disillusion
A broken heart
Beyond repair.

And there is one more
The one who sees
Hate and passion
As relations
Hate to deliver heavy blows
Passion to put hot pepper
In calm eyes.

As for me
Loneliness is my
Companion in the
House of rains
Not the wetness of
Urine and maggots
But the coldness of
One
Living with oneness
Wailing
Sobbing
Just as others cry.

Disincarnation

He sees another life
Where the angels will wake him
The saints serve him breakfast
Nuns kiss and ask for more
Another life!

But this is not his reincarnated life
As he fears he may come back
Once again
As him
That him
Whose face is afraid to see.

What he wants is that other life
The one before this one
Where he was told
That he once presided over an empire
An empire made in heaven
Where his name was one:
Oracle.

The Chameleon

Yesterday he sought change
The predictability of change
Reconciliation with the past
A charged past
A burning fire
To quench optimism
In the flame of hesitancy

Today he seeks renewal
The unpredictability of a future
Fast asleep in a bed
Of uncertainties
Calmness at bay
Blind faith

Tomorrow will be normal
If normal means abnormality
In the sadness of eternity
The agelessness of despair
The nightmares of tiredness

A frightening day after
In the planet of loneliness
Unshared tears
In a garden
Full of thorns
He fails to cry
Remembering only yesterday
To think of tomorrow
The oddity of the abnormal

Pain

I am hit by pain
Not the trauma of conscience
Or the struggle to do right
Not of that dirty mind
Roaming in darkness
I am not running away
From errors of yesteryear
Fighting my past

I am struck by agony
Not from the fullness
Of my cup of iniquities
The faucet of my shame
Nor thoughts of suicide

Pain has visited
My body today
I weep
My head a battlefield
Watery eyes
Mucus nose
The brain and legs
At war
Veins of the heart
Broken
Fluids exhausted
Stomach on the verge
Of explosion
I suffocate
I am choking
Vanishing breath
Help!
My boat is sinking
I am drowning
I taste it
Yes
The brine of the
Unknown.

Departure

Multiple tasks
Diversified energies
Transient pursuit of dreams
With eyes wide open
Wobbling legs
Along unsteady paths of discovery.

Pensive moods
Inkless pens
Paperless tables
Floating ideas
Like broken calabashes on the sea.
Mounted hands
Trapped in a procrastinated body.

Formidable lover
Dear damsel
Daughter of Fate
Drawn to epic battles
With the little woman
    the nocturnal deer
     troubled by headlights
In the calligraphy of affection
Cheer, cheer, cheer
The beer is cold.

The jaguar sleeks
From city to village
Carrying all
But the death certificate.

Vile odors of comrades
Brown cauldron of betrayal
Rumbled bellies of soulless minds
Spineless as fishes
Flexible in character
Fillets of migraine
Pounding the head to crumbles
Keep marching, comrade, in
Pools of strange
Concoction.

Go, friend, go
Glide on
To kindred colors
Primal valleys
A journey of no return.

Passage to India

She heard she came from India
She dreamt of India
Not in India
Out of India
In the city of rains

She saw India
In an Indian
Decked in
Long hair
Bohemian pants
Big teeth
Indian heart

She wanted the Indian
Horrendous desires
Forcing the door open
Discovering a cave
Hiding the Indian

And there came darkness
The Indian kept snoring
She kept awake
Frozen by the secrets of the past
She remembered
One Indian had discarded her
Another Indian had collected her

She saw another Indian
In the theater of darkness
She wore a crown of thorns
Blood dripping
Drenched
She fled to heat

Stabbed by another Indian
She escaped
To a faraway land
The real India
Away from the fake

Revenge

I first met him
When my legs found themselves
In that strange and ancient land
A force to be reckoned with
I heard he once defeated
An army of miscreant demons
Single-handedly
But he was kind, too
Gentle in his own way
Although his eyes
Kept their one true color:
Red.

When I asked about his name
He laughed inscrutably
But without malice
Instead of answering
He sliced open a coconut
And everything
Or so I thought
Was sealed.

Only much later
When I had cause to visit
His abandoned home
Did I understand
Here, indeed, was a warrior
Descended from the land of mines
Expelled by land grabbers
Burrowed, he lamented
Furrowed, he energized.

Obsession followed
Strange recitations
Birthing energies
To fight
As he proclaimed
Those who take all:
    Plasma of power
    Juice of money
    Milk of land
Then did he declare his war
A war without end.

Austin's July

I step outside
To run inside
To escape an oven
Ready to roast my head
Tears of expectation
Not for revolution
Not for reform
But for one small gift:
    Rain

I curse the dust
It rises again
To tan my body
I make one plea:
    Rain, fall on me!

I hear thunder
I rejoice
The clouds darken
I clap
I tell the brown grass
To expect its food
When a new earth will
Reveal its harvest
The thunder leaves
The clouds break
Rainbows take a vacation
Rain stays away
The season keeps its faith:
    Worship me, it says
    Today and tomorrow.

PART B

Reflections of Agonies

Torture

Pain, a routine
Pain, a paycheck
The training manual of pain

Pain performs its unquestioning duty
Unquestions that cannot find
    the unanswers of dignity
    the unsecrets of hope
    the unlocations of love
    the untime of memory

The brave to be broken
Bravery not to hold the citadel
But to accept the work
Of keeping the heart's fullness still
Remaining watchful of past and future.
In those last, long days
The brave have their tears.

The deadly genius
To discover the last shelters
    Beat the flesh
    Twist the limbs
    Burn the skin
    Break the bones
    Gouge the eyes
    Rape the sex
    Relish the screams
Humiliate the innocence of self protection
Confound the preciousness of self respect
Drain the last drops of the persistent spirit.

I yield
Take even this
Take all you can
All is not taken

The excruciating alchemy of pain
    the individual
    the singular
    the small man
    the defenseless woman
Shattered to release the collective treasure –
The mingling of love
The unbroken flight of strength
The spirit dancing
In the luminous fecundity of tradition
Your pain cannot touch our dead!

Pain is a foolish colonizer
No longer a new enemy
Pain is defanged
Tamed, a small ugly pet
Ferocious still in its new cage.

You cannot defeat us
You cannot destroy justice
You can only defile justice.

Shock and Awe

My master
I live in peace
With swords and spears
Enough to keep
Zealous neighbors at bay
My oil I cannot drink
Gold I have none
My golden oil you crave
To mobilize the army
Replacing machines
To drill
As they kill

Bring them on!
Your bombardment
Doesn't cease
You hunt for the living
In a game of smoke
Seeking neither peace
Nor surrender
Collateral damage dumped
In shallow graves of sand
The slaves must soon reply
To expand the vocabulary
Of nationalism to
Nukular

State Violence

The police is lawful
The army fateful
The executioner does his work
To remove one creation
From the universe
Uncreated by all
    State violence

Swords soaked in blood
Flooded rivers of blood
The rage of political players
To enrage the citizens of hope
    State violence

Chief President
Whose law
What law
Why law
Do you make
To quench the sadistic hunger
For blood
Drink!
Redded teeth
    State violence

Our wreaths are too many
Fresh remembrances
Scattered as dust
From corners to crannies
We weep to weep
    State violence

Strong Generals
Commandants of woes
Great tormentors
Keeping all as bondage
Medals of gore
Honor conferred
On the wicked
By the crooked
    State violence

The poor
Enemy power of the good
Liquidated for the glory of the bad
To build a land of the worse
Uncooked carcasses
To feed the eyes of the mighty
    State violence

Imperialism

Strong states attack the weak
Blaming them for inviting
Invasion as
Big fish eat the small
Guns trained and honed to kill
Debasing honest protection.

Civilize them!
Their smell too odious
Their fate sealed in the
Contract of oblivion.
Confiscate their land
They die of hunger
Plant food for other lands
Take all
For they deserve none
Genocide
Wasted lives
Gasping and groping
Awaiting the verdict
Of hell delivered
By a new God.

Collective misfortunes
Streets of suffering
Dotting dusted terrains
Tribes and tongues collapse
Into oblivion and abyss.

Hatred sown
Germinating self destruction
Hearty stalks of violence
Harvested with death.

Outrage!
Wars without mandate
Untamed armies
Parading with blades and stones
Guns and broken bottles
Seeking revenge
Tasting blood.

Purified anger
To cleanse psyches
Scarred by violence
Irritated eyes of bitterness
Tongues of venom
Clenched fists
Relaxing to cast heavy stones
To crush the skulls of
Vengeful enemies.

Genocide

Rivers of Rwanda transubstantiated, a dark dye
The arteries of the Niger Delta clogged with dead blood
Red flooding through the streets of the Sudan
Kosovo, the red rains not forgotten
The oppression of the poor
Is the chorus of the songs
Of iniquity and injustice.

History runs amok
The thunder of power
Triggering troubles
Massacres
Spreading fears
Anxieties
A flood of dead bodies
Washed into shallow waters.

Papa's land
Now soldier's land
Desolate land
Emptied of people
Trees, animals
Communities raped and routed
To honor the gods
Of greed.

Ominous clouds
Frightened minds
Silenced mouths
Awaiting their end
At the hands of
The liquidators
Patriotic bandits
Enlightened marauders.

The Maradona of Politics

He dribbles the people
Our people
To perpetuate himself in
Power
Shameless leader
Making our people
Tenants in their own lands
Believer in human rights
While the prisons are filthy full
Of men of conscience.
He can spell freedom
But the press must salute
Cautious collaborators
To ridicule critics
Azeri is small before you
Kasparov can be defeated
The oracle, lawmaker
Always to be applauded
To escape the iron cuffs.

Chaos and confusion
Sources of smiles
For the Great Leader
Debauchery and rape
Written on the coat of arms
Inexorable force of one
The national pledge
His patrimony
A huge asylum
In a dry land
Of vanishing dreams.

Dribble on, Maradona
Beastly neck
Disfigured hands
Fast legs
Blinded eyes
A mouth crowded with noise
Dead ears
Worthless face
The Gates of Hell
Never close.

Hegemonic Culture

The universal peacock
Dancing for all to see
Songs of arrogance
Drums of shame
Sneering myopia
A peacock in red feathers

Flapping its stench
From colorful gowns
The boastful peacock
    enforcing distance
    ransoming our mother
    bulldozing our home

The peacock travels
On a lonely path
Destination: Division
    internalized racism
    intentional calamities
    preemptive wars

The peacock frowns
Belly bloated with sweat
Uneasy welcome
Unfriendly introductions
The peacock is imperious
    lacking subtlety
    rejecting ambiguity
    dead movements
    cheap horizons

The peacock struts aloof
Untouchably silked
And gold plated
Unattainable
Inscrutable object of desire
Alas, of identification

The tightening tenacity of
Stumbles in a static life
Spare the peacock
Understand the arrogance
    to dismantle violent truths
    to navigate cultural difference
    to inaugurate dialogue

The peacock is not a trader
Its bright feathers unsaleable
Look again
Not all is for profit
The peacock is different from you
    complacent separation
    frozen dominance
    fragmented values

Move slowly
Touch the peacock
Transcend your cage
Shed only little of your skin
Review the peacock
Inspect yourself
The double vision
Of the hegemonic
And your striving authenticity
Is dynamic marginality
A potent becoming
    now
    later

You know too much
Losing our culture
Emulating the peacock
Until it's too late
To remember the original look.
How do we return
To activate our old,
When the peacock has become a ghost?

77

From Round Rock to Palestine

Roaring like a lion
Off he went
From Round Rock
To the war zone
In the East of the Middle
The middle of muds
In waters of anarchy

Imaginary escape
To the real morass
Big sores to heal
The holes got bigger

An open sore
Lanced with mockery
Lullabies of gunfire
In slaughtered lands
Flooded with tears
He remembered Round Rock
But forgot to throw
The rocks in his pocket
Eclipsing himself with
Revolutionary words

A dangling noose appeared
His neck was ready
The noose came nearer
His head enlarged
Too large to take the rope
The clarion call:
Open the prison gates!

The world shouted
Keyboards put to work
To internetize the
Pregnancy
A hemorrhage
Then a stillborn
Delivered at Round Rock
A cry here
A cry there
Undoctored wounds
In the muds of the middle east.

Primal World

Our population a mystery not
Our geography we knew enough
In the land we claimed
Yet unknown to eaters of the world
Bringing us the fruits and grass to devour
A full stomach, a merry mind.

The umbrella of trees
Smoke sauntering from the pipes below
The birds hovering above
Singing to proclaim the majesty
Beyond the cloud
Our land of wonder.

Fire of warmth
Mouth agape with freshness
As the campfire works its miracles
Miracles of heat, fires of passion
Warmth of hearts.

Crabs walk yonder beyond
Edges of rivers to toy and play
Campfire dreams
Of roasted crabs in company
In the land of balance
Our wonder land.

Route to Roots

The posters hang
Displaying the wishes of the new
They cover the old
Hanging
Like the rope of suicide.

Look back!
The gadgets speak to their world
Killing the elders with the moonlight
Stories of you
Now roasted
In the microwaves of globalization.

The heat suffocates
History no longer cools
Languages talk not
And culture sleeps.

Where am I?
In the womb of emptiness
A broken unity
Of nothing to become
I must travel back in time
To find other posters.

Red and Black

Can I not name myself?
You call me what you like
Africa today, nigger tomorrow
Nigger, Nègre, Neg
The red of yesterday, the tan of today
Or am I the red-black?

I am in you!
The apes that became human
Populating the earth before the codes
You are in me!
Your mulatto's old and new.

A drop of blood is the marrow in the iron chain
In the genes of history
The veins remain
The vehicles of ancestries
Of the natives, free, colored, enslaved, unchained
My blood is not extinct.

Call me names
Unmixed negroid
Molato, Mulatow, Mulato, Muletto, Mulo, Mule
Negroes of the Indians
Americans of the Africans
Natives of the Blacks
Unions of the impossible
Intermixtures of the curious
The curious of the anonymous
I am in you!

From Slavery to Slavery

Uprooted from far away
In chains across the ocean
The sea of sickness
Journeys of pains
Frowning faces
Forever crying
Lamenting their past
Regretting their present

The past remembered
Of dealers who stole their children
Freighting them, as they feared
Through tunnels of horror
Faces and faeces
Mixed in ships of horror
To destinations of hell
Where sadistic masters
Turned some into concubines
Others into petty workers
In hot plantations
Uprooted from their base
With new names
In places unknown
They cried in anger
No peace in sight
Until they lost their sight
Discarded into stinking pits

They cried more
For lost gods
Stolen by invaders
Selling new faith
With decrees:
    burn your symbols
    abandon your kinship
    take other names
    wear these clothes
    eat this food
They obeyed
To lose faith
To lose land
To lose face

The present remembered
They cry yet more
With no reason to rejoice
Too many taxes
To feed the rich
Too many laws
To rob them of land
Too many guns and batons
To coerce submission
Too many regulations
To tie their tongues
Too much work
To break their backs
Too many debts
To send them to the graves
Where there will be no eyes
To cry.

Bread and Bullets

He asked for bread
You gave him bullets
His decomposed body
Food for vultures and dogs
In the land of sorrow and blood

The bloodlust of the
AK 47 to hide the
Cowardice of power
Conmen craving more
Nicotine of force
To eradicate the
Living dead

Corpses litter the ground
The bondage of
Blood and sport
The spirits cry:
Witches, face
The Inquisition
Justice from the graves
Before the Day of Judgment
The sooner the hellfire
The longer the roast

Frantz Fanon

Prophets never die
Only sleep
For us to whisper.

We talk
As our prophet sleeps
Dreaming of shame
Inflicted upon him
By non-dreamers.

Prophet, be asleep
See no more visions
As little remains
But collapsing pillars
Of houses of straw.
Disciples of yesteryear
In your trenches of battle
Now dine with the enemy
To torture
The pennynaires
With stolen power
To starve the foot soldiers.

Our land, no longer green
The ravages you saw
By savages from abroad
Our wallets
Now emptied
By the keepers of records.

A burden to ourselves
We remain victims
As the Prophet foretold
Of the locusts
Eating up the land.
Sleep, wake no more
To escape
Death
From kith and kin.

Counter Violence

Terrorist today
Nationalist tomorrow
As Nelson Mandela
Walks magically
From Prison to
State House

Electoral justice
Killed with overstuffed
Ballot boxes
Decaying houses of chads

Rush to the judges
Big bellies
Calculators of manipulation
Manipulators of calculation
Presiders over gluttony
The lurid robes of filth and carcass

Managers talk of order
Be fair to us
We are fair to you
Counting all the votes
Listening to complaints
The system has regulations
Remember?

Confused rulers
Managers of damage
Seated on the thrones
Sanctified by boxes and judges
To administer chaos
Demoncracy, the
Militocracy of
Dollarmaniacs

Let my people go
Far away from the
Barracks of torture
Palaces of orgies
Houses of deception

I am enchained
Blind my eyes
To see the skeletons in
Your cupboard of iniquities

I know you
We are many
Too many to count
You are few
Too few to see
As evil
In human skins

Call me the masses
First name: masses
Last name: masses
Masses Masses
You cannot know
Uncountable grains of sand

The masses are fed
Fed, with anger
Fed, with lies
Enough to destroy
Ballot boxes
That produce results
Of demonism

The sovereignty of the poor
To release the chains
The governance of the poor
To dismantle
The house of horror

The battle lines are drawn
We are sworn enemies
In the great divide
Foes forever
Until we speak a new language:
Vox Populi
Vox Del.

Quiet Work

How can I become quiet
About my momentous work
Telling just a few
Not to seek celebration
Or an award unannounced
But sharing my movement
To invite accompaniment

To move writing
Beyond an exercise
I must remain quiet
    to witness the fractures at my feet
    to conjure the solid ground of the future
    to fulfill the urgency of recording
    to order the frenzy of my brain
    to silence doubters far and near
    to respect the enigmas of effort
    to enable work

When the silence is broken
Spatters of rain
Will fill the earth
Cooling the land
Irrigated minds
Will gather
To honor
The new sounds

Brilliance

He hit his head on his desk
As he bowed before the screen.
An accident created by
Great thoughts
Traveling diametrically from
His wishes, his real wishes
Creating imaginary
Ethnographic inscriptions.

Wishes fighting brilliance
One spoofs the protocols of secularity
The other of insularity
His wishes define the limits of
Transmigration, the pitfalls of
Transnationalism.

The restless mind wonders
Doubting brilliance:
Its Oedipal nature
Imposed authority
Of patriarchy's resonance
The cold brutality of ideas.

Notes litter the floor
Fieldnotes, headnotes
An archive of memory
Scraps of papers
Bonded to produce
Musings on
Faraway places.

The brilliance celebrates
The absolute difference of his wishes
The deviation from the path of traditionalism
The difference inscribed into deviance
Of human interactions.
Wishes and brilliance
Merged at last!
His head can now hit the desk
So the blood can fill the pen.

B.A., M.A., Ph.D.

No matter the new revelations
And new failures
Brilliance will not take
You and me
Out of this place
To a just society
Instead, efforts of living
Forces of regularity
More powerful than diplomas.

Marx is brilliant
    no more than me
But wise enough to do one thing:
Converse with the past
To meditate on the present.
New insights cannot derail Marx
Even when doubters
Presume to transcend
Those ideas of old.

The solution is never a formula,
Frozen in rigid filaments
Locate the ideas
Unchain the souls
Analysis alone
Frees no one
Robe the body in the garment
Made of purpose.

Write
Think
The unfolding of time
Contains the secrets
To save agitated minds.
Speak
Speak well
The tasks of the present
Salvage potent words of knowledge
Rich visions and values
    containing energies
    illustrating balance
    inaugurating deployment
    revealing intensities

Offer listeners
Darkness and light
Laughter and words.

Despair not of
Anguish buried in speech.
The book can talk
Forcing the witnesses to talk back.
The listener becomes the book
To be read with respect,
The length of time
Gracing the listener
With the invocation of speech.

The long horizon
Cradles the short moment,
Each breath
The mouth opens the word
    manifest the intervention
    activate the books with speech
    tame the journals with presence
To allow sparks to flower.

Heads of diamond
Shaping fingers of poison.
Beware
Retool
Wisdom exceeds brilliance
Roles of force and visibility
    empowering the diplomas
    supplying the fuel
    transforming our lives
Traces of originality
Inscribed in
    new books
    new questions
The capacity to walk with integrity.

Postcoloniality

Hybridity of the embedded
Enlightenment of the periphery
Bildungsroman without the Caesar
Addressing problems without theories
Poems without images
Narrow discussions of identity
Troubling the narrow-minded.

Engagements without faith
Hard texts, unreadable lines
Crevices of troubles
Capturing historical moments
The riddles of cultural difference
Grasping for the scarce ethical.

May the next generation
Transcend the old bewilderments
My project, my worries.
But my generation is embedded
In the intimate snares of history
Reveal
Conceal
Discover
Whatever the truths
And falsehoods
Turn out to be.

My wheel lies under
Waiting for me to reinvent
Earned triumphs
Honorable failures
Lamented retreats
Work
More work
Our genius.

Intellectualizing

Techne glides into
The crowded room of isms
Rejoicing with *episteme*.
In the elegance of language
Episteme befriends *techne*
With the knowledge of proportion.

Epistemetechne
A compact rhythm
You sound so powerful and charming
Dance with my dilemmas:
     becoming an intellectual
     solving problematics
     answering cultural crises
     memorizing volumes
     divorcing the learned from the practical.

Answer me, oh *techne*
Betray me not, oh *episteme*
Give salvation
Stand not in the way
Banish not the intellectual
Subordinate the intellectual, yes,
To practice the needs of living.

Gurus

Commitment of the learned
Drawing from our sources
Rich heritage
Wells of tradition
Mastery of multiple sites
Diverse histories
Moving us forward
Producing force and effects
Offering us legitimacy.

Incarnate intellectuals
Guru figures
Experts
Breaking
The boundaries of ideas
Birthing new meanings
Defeating old models.

Subjects of emulation
In worlds of deterioration
Corrupted by faltering words.
The politics of intellectual work
Is never satisfied
By the purity of thought
Or by its
    conceptualization
    composition
    dissemination
Relevance springs
From specificity
Localized knowledge
Grounded experience
Intersections of
Concept and flesh
And the worldly force exerted
By thinking.

Children of the Diaspora

Far from home,
The undefined homeland
Recognizable in the unconscious
Clothes become costumes
Garb on top of spiced stomachs.

We gather yet again
Bonded by roots
Tied to an unknown future –
Neeru from the land beyond the skies
Akhila from the land beyond the sea.

The diaspora talks back
Discourses of desire
Furious intensity
Words claiming self
Speeches of clarity
Offered with alacrity.

Shame covers our faces
Blooded faces
Of masks hiding spirits
Unmask!
Shout your presence
Protest the denigration
Of the innocent land.

The host is a shark
Ready to swallow
Resist
Fight
Understand the waters.

Innocent children
Devouring the treacherous bananas
Brainwashed
Programmed to
Celebrate destruction.

Retool the brains
Blame not the innocent
Assaulted by idle chatter
Hammer the nails of truth
Secure the strength
Uncork the bottles of action
And unleash vibrant desires.

You, Me, and Us

You need me
I seek you
All of us
A united audience
for ourselves
The We locked with the Me.

I seek more relations
to comprehend myself
    our identities
    our experience
    our purpose
The family as audience
inaugurating the Self
Public images and stories
painting us in sticky hues
Teachers, classmates
contributing to the mix.

Eclipsed by slumber
Forgotten before my burial
In the midst of an audience
with its engines
of othering
and indifference
Flights for my imagination
in chasing my destiny.

Try me!
Close the ranks
in order to see:
    beauty
    value
    uniqueness
    complexity
    richness
    traditions
    intensity
    entitlement
I will be receptive to you
whether
you receive me
or not.

A New Compass

Minor discoveries
Of an unrecoverable life
Creating the big bang
Bringing rushes of emotion
Of astonishment
As he digests the text
Of a lost past.

A lost past?
With a memory renewed?
Of humbling gestures?
Of words of honor?
Relentless gratitude
Thinking backward
To see the forward
Grounded in the axis of liberation.

A rooted traditionalist in India?
A nationalist in Africa?
An uprooted traditionalist in London?
A modernizer in the Golden Gates?
A postcolonialist in Austin?
Who knows?
Only he who can define.

Divine Revelations

Forty days and forty nights
I stayed in the wilderness
Angel Gabriel did not show up
Maybe no one has seen the Angel
Only fabricated stories
Frightening sinners to follow.

I left the wilderness
I kept quiet
Not for the sake of celebration
since I saw no angel
But to explore
myself, something
beyond myself
The flowering of a destiny.

I think I understand
The embodiment of force
The unleashing of forces
    through engagement
    the acquisition of roles
    the enactment of obligations
Something takes place
Something remains quiet!

The Prophet's thirteen disciples
do not realize
Even the Prophet is not aware
of the ground that enables his work
The Prophet thinks he is god
Knowing the why
of his doing
Escaping hell
Dominating Satan.

I think I know
There is a ground
of cultural coherence
A dynamic horizon of tradition
that animates the Prophet
that feeds breath to his work.

I am a disciple
Weak searcher of a message
Confused words
Vexed actions
As I look
To the fractures in the ground.

To what end?
To bear witness to the fractured ground
Of my inaction
To create a new ground
With earnest features
Not fully visible or spoken.

Sexuality 101

The gregarious laughter of men
    the boastful vie for attention
    the quiet smile, knowing hearts
    the untested may be eager or shy
    the cruel and careless rejoice in knowing how to take
    the hospitable and kind assure the balance.

The wise boisterousness of women
    the ribald songs before marriage
    the outlandish pour dancing heat from eyes and limbs
    the astonished are quick to dispel their dismay
    the resigned and the starved feed the embers aglow again
    unknown yearnings a called forth to sing.

Laughter taunts the laughless boy
Blinklessly bewildered
Eager to join their delight
But frozen by obscure troubles past
Fearful for others to listen
Startling his own shadow with
The ponderous weight of his woes.

Don't laugh
Your joke is my ridicule
One day, I will laugh with you.

Sexuality: First Steps

Memory one is the Grade 6
girl who phoned
    a gesture sweet
    a nervous step
    a brief exchange
followed only by
some ribbing
from the vacation uncle.

The step was not false,
my desire awakening to
the thought of another
liking me
at the ready age of 10.

Desire kindled in Grade 7
beholding
the sparkling cheerleader
and the retiring pompom girl,
the fateful launching
of Distant Dreams.

Fantasy awaited in Grade 8,
the unspoken yearning for
my very own girl
flourishing on
the overnight school trip.

They looked at me
and I at them.
What did they see in
this mutual yet unequal look?
I could hardly fathom
I stood before
the unending enchantment
of femininity.

The search for recognition
mixed with
a confining fear.
I never knew that
this is when
boys scramble
to conquer.

Were girls my benefactors
constraining
the bullying of boys?
But then a fight
with another boy
before a crowd:
a quick defeat
my tearful lonely
turn to home
a spectacle indeed.

A girl chased after me,
my glasses in her hand.
With pained hostility
I waved away her gesture
And off she ran
the limits of her
young generosity reached,
glasses on the grass.

To see and to be seen:
A turning point
False steps began
Mistrusting lenses spying
rejection and betrayal.
Oh, teach me to beat the boys
to regain the courage of desire.

Sexuality: Second Steps

I must become a man
I must stand up
Learn to fight those
Who humiliate me
But I am no fighter!
Too gentle
Too empathic
Too stupid.

Other talents unfolded
Mastering numbers
Mastering words
Sufficient devices
For keeping
Concerned eyes
At bay.

And yet there was she
Who inspired reveries sweet
Reverent longing
Affectionate admiration
The faithful secret
She became
In distance
A comforting familiar
Part of myself
A self-created world of
Wistful belonging.

The Spanish teacher
Showed us that film with
Only the third breast I'd ever seen
A raucous older woman
Giving the bewildered boy suck.

My cocooning desire sought
The city's underworld
I, a boy
Seeking to see
Seeking to talk
Seeking to touch
In the cabarets of
Emboldened innocence.

Sexuality: The Multiplication

I have come to conquer a national territory.
Desire, my instrument of conquest and invitation:
    the outlandish ornament of my youth
    the irresistible charm of my masculinity
    the sacred engine of creation and fulfillment.

To include or to be included, that is the question.
I was destined to be a high priest of compassion,
Performing the grand rituals of acknowledgment,
A man making women feel alive and significant,
One whose tenderness is received as gift,
Lending the weight of righteousness to trembling hearts.

In the midst of my opulence you will find a fervent secret:
My terror of speaking the need for belonging in an alien land,
Desire transmuting to shame –
    the cowardice of restraint
    the disenfranchisement of potency
    the chosen exile of delay.

I am a laughable conqueror
Without army, without weapons
    Reluctant to compete
    Perplexed by antagonism
    Pained by dismissal
An unprepared understudy lost in longing,
Culpably innocent in the minefields of desire.

Desire could have been a luscious flame,
Happily roasting myself and others.
I have journeyed from prince and priest
To needy bastard, an ordinary sunovabitch,
Graceless hawker of his cheapened wares.
I can see the altering lines of my face
The winsome smile and generous eyes
Giving way to the stern determination
Of a beggar's yearning.

The friction of arousal –
My encircling arm
The fragrant billow of her hair
Her hands reaching to discover me
Cushions of flesh amid humid entanglement.

The fiction of acceptance –
Hungering for surfaces,
The limitless feminine
Turned into scarce resource.
Women as passports
Rarely valid beyond a night.
Border crossings without direction
Vanishing inscriptions
Doomed repetitions.

These nights of paucity haunt my dignity
Spill poison on my honorable work
Catapult me to a pauper's land,
Wretched residence for dwarfed spirits.

Again, with fallen heart
And undocumented desire,
Discounting the treasures of home,
I heed the call of the erotic multitudes,
Seeking receptive smiles
And hospitable flesh.

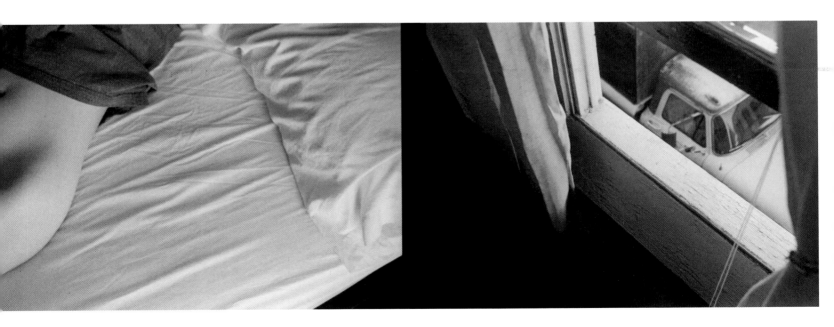

Hit The Road!

Beauty and Brains
Combined in
Elegant simplicity in
The lady from the Plains
Joyous, ethical
Her man, a dreamer
Holding love,
The diamond of hope,
The gold of lust
He prefers

She, waiting, rusting
Unsure passage of time
Shrinking her breasts
Tallness shortened
Fat skimmed
Color ruptured
Her man laughed
Handicapped on Sunday
Artless on Monday
Pompous on Tuesday
Nasty on Wednesday
Careless on Thursday
Hopeless on Friday
Suicidal on Saturday

She was dismayed
Confusing him with Christ
Peace and godliness from the desert
To transform her
He was no Christ
The creator
Caring about womankind
Fire can ravage his house
His tower can collapse
His burning logs can turn to ashes
His gazelle can fall prey to bullets
As he hits the road
Leaving disaster behind
To face the tragic

Jamaica Comes, Goes

The potent radiance of the day
Shines forth from her
The umbrella of dreads
Sheltering her
Announcing wonders

Their brave and pained paths met
At the crossroads of conviction
His desire: excellence
Her goal: creativity
Success seekers
In a world
Without traditions

The anarchy of freedom
Reigns
Men's power
Women's liberation
All right, all wrong
With love
In between

Love in a season of failures
Questions become arrows
Shot at doubting chests
Thundering disbeliefs
Echoes of pouncing fears
Routes of guarded retreat

She called it quits
Running away from faith
Venturing to another fate
Far from him
Who thinks not of tomorrow

Bus 5

Living was I, at Popolo
In transit from love
To affairs
All sorts and heights
Entangled relations
Indebtedness aplenty

Venturing forth
Myself become a fiend
Tormented by my demons
Chasing me as I chase them
Lonely in the beds of many
Swimming in the pool
Of sorrow

I dreamt of salvation
Of one love
By my side
One home
Only she and him
The Honey of Sweetheart

The love came
Soon enough
Before you blinked
In Bus number 5
Traveling to Popolo
and beyond
To a new land

The moment of passion
Arrived as fire
Burning my heart
Consuming my desire
Quenching my lusts
And defeating my infatuations

Let Popolo pass today
I will travel further
Body temperature rising
Love in the marrow
Jealousy creeps in
As I want no one
Near my destiny

My honey left the bus
I became the bees
A new source of honey
I followed
Exploding ecstasy
Bold, I request
Like instant coffee
A time to start
A new path of life
On broad roads
Leading from Popolo
She assented
A body of iron
Soon to become
Molten fragrance

The Lion and the Deer

Her night, blinded by day
Wide awake at night
She imagines herself a lion
A threatened lion
Roaring
To instill fear
In the heart of the only deer
Roaming in the small cage

A cage for two
Low light, dim shadows
The lion, hungry
The deer, running
Restless days
Treacherous nights

The deer grows wings
Flying to safety high in the cage
In a zone of sanity
Where it must hang
Never to descend
Trapped in a cage
Legs turning to rock

The lion waits
In an unhomely space
Of gloom and doom
Estranged from power
Dispossessed of prey
The king of animals
Now hunting herself

Two thoughtless souls
One suspended in air
The other starving to death
Wasted energies
In the shelters of misfortune
In the solace of hunger

Lightening struck!
The world rumbled
Unearthly sounds
The cage opened
The lion expelled
To nowhere
The deer fallen
Unable to walk
Silence!
Uneasy ease
Hisses, curses
Curses, hisses

The End of Prologues

Let me hear before I begin
What I should know
So that I can plan to see
What lies ahead
Though I reserve the right
To look back like the one
Who once lost faith.

Forget the prologue!
The preface be damned!
Put the foreword to sword!
Leap to your feet
The lake is the ocean
There is no assignment
When the destination is now.

The music is pleasant sweet
But I've been seduced before.
State the motive
And I'll test the waters
My toe, not Achilles' heel.
I cherish the wisdom of caution
The joy of anticipation.

The prologue waits and watches.
She observes the others dance,
Cool vacant valleys
Wildly filling
With spirit and fire.
Claim them within yourself
As you take stage to instigate life.

I am the marketplace of options
The bricolage of identities.
I traverse modernities of surface
Back to traditions of depth.
O, devour this ardent war
Between sacred and
Phantasmal pleasures.

Queen Compulsion,
You are border and symbol
When wilt thou command thyself?
Writing precedes
The prologue of reading.
The Prince has fallen
Bid him rise in love.

The Detached Suitor

The problem with detachment, you see, is that it all sounds very well and good in theory.
Let's see how it works in metaphor.

Let's say, for example, that on this side of the stage we have a mango,
Bursting with the fullness of his own destiny and generosity.
He offers himself to the world without any expectation,
The life force flowing through him,
Sparkles of hope giving shape to honest intentions and contented feelings.
Such a selfless offering of self is its own reward.

Okay, so the mango is sitting there, calmly expressing his true nature.
In tune with his own destiny, he doesn't ask anyone to validate him, to fulfill his purpose.
Indeed, the mango is feeling downright philosophical.
As it turns out, just across the way, on the other side of the stage, is a mouth,
An especially ravishing one, if you must know.
The mango imagines the mouth luxuriating in discovering his heart,
Coordinating her lips and teeth and tongue for maximum pleasure and fulfillment.
But the mouth isn't paying any attention to the mango.
Perhaps she isn't hungry, or she's distracted by something else.
Perhaps the mouth doesn't even know what she wants.

Well, the mango weighs these various possibilities, and remains steadfast and patient,
Even though it's fairly obvious to everyone that the mango and mouth are perfect for one another.
And so the mango takes a deep, meditative breath,
And continues to express himself as poignant, artistic gesture, an emblem of creation.

But then, the mango can't help fretting.
The mouth *must* see him.
Why, in the name of God, doesn't she just grab him, squeeze him,
Devour him, the rich juices flowing like tears of reunited love?
I mean, can we blame the mango for being a bit frustrated or dejected, even deflated?
His opening presentation of self was an honest and dignified one.
Surely, that should have meant something to the mouth.
Could he have been so wrong about her and/or himself?
Is it fair to ask the mango, expressing his highest nature,
To consider so many questions and doubts?
All he wanted was to offer himself nobly,
Providing nourishment, delivering delight, not seeking anything in return.
And then, on top of all this, there's the business of the other mangoes.

[continued]

Does the mouth have her eye on one of them instead?
The mango doesn't have anything against them.
They are his brothers, after all, and he's not one to be jealous.
He's sure that the other mangoes must also have their own noble gestures and purposes,
Or, at the very least, their perfectly legitimate self interests.
They may not be as glorious as he.
Actually, he hasn't wanted to think in those competitive terms.
He just wants to be himself, and he really does want what's best for others.

The mango tries to remain brave in his own innocence.
No one told the mango anything about the temporality of detachment!
You can't just achieve it, you have to sustain it.
Yet the knowledge that the world is a colder, more calculating place
Is seeping into the mango's consciousness.
Now, when this mouth, or another mouth, finally does decide to give the mango a go,
Will this awareness of the world's indifferent complexity have seeped into his flesh?
What will be the flavor, then, of the mango's noble gestures?

For a while, the mango considers shouting out to the mouth.
Part of him almost believes that she would be convinced,
That she would see him as he sees himself, selfless and unassuming.
But the mango refrains, respecting the mouth's right to choose.
He feels the rejection in the pit of his stomach.
Shouldn't the mouth at least say something, offer some kind of explanation?
Alas, the greatest blow to detachment is indifference.

The mango remembers again the joy and truth of his ripe and juiceful self.
Ultimately, he's willing to be detached by the weight of his own overripe fullness,
Turning into mango wine, crushed beneath feet rather than honored with a mouthly death.
The mango plumps his soul, liberated and unapologetic,
And tries to forget the agony of waiting.

PART C

Transcending Agonies

Tribute to Our Elder

Live to a ripe old age
To acquire a cognomen
Like those before you.
On the day we age
When we grow old
A righteous time
The day of wisdom
Our friends will call us
In praise.

Our elder
Let us praise you
Now we accept you
You are an elder
Today you grow old
Today you become wise
This righteous day
We praise you
With a new title
The Chief of the Kingdom of Peace.

Darkness radiates the forest
    with esteem
Roundness adorns the hill
    with joy
Our elder
The Chief of the Kingdom of Peace
Delivers history
    with passion
Keep talking, Chief
Go the way of the stirring stick.

Swift as a hawk
One who hunts like a cat
Chief, the Kingdom shall not fall
Transmigrate
Retain the spirit in the Kingdom
Our elder
Your Kingdom will not fall.

The Teacher

Good morning, class.
Good morning, Ms. Saraswati.
Now, class, what did we learn yesterday?
We learned that $2 + 2$ doesn't always equal 4.
That's right, Rohan, very good.
Anjali, do you have a question?
Yes, Ms. Saraswati, what did you mean by
"Embracing the wisdom of contradiction"?

I have wondered about her
When we're not there.
Who is she for herself?
Her mind's hunger
Her heart's beat
Her body stretched towards life.

"I don't think you have the luxury of self-pity!"
She dispels nonsense with a flourish.
She rewards only our true effort
Born of trusting ourselves,
Doing our dirt work.
She doesn't ask that we impress her
But that we surprise ourselves.

I should not be jealous of her other people.
Her royal azure gold
    Floating
    Alighting
    Mingling
Taking joy in joy
Honoring sorrow
Releasing rubies of mischief.
I'll bet she doesn't suffer fools,
Wielding her weapons
Against mediocrity and cowardice.

The bell rings
She glances at the clock
Her giving gaze fixes us again
We're not yet dismissed.

I have grown up with her
She watched
She clapped
She admonished
She grinned.
And may she know love
And may she have beauty
And may her iridescence find mirror.

The Departed Comrade

The halls of Justiceville are dark today
    but the light shines on
The halls of Justiceville are uneasy today
    but their steadiness is ensured
The halls of Justiceville are sad today
    but the joy is deep.

The comrade travels on
Having done her work.
Countless duties and efforts
A lifetime of devoted service
How many lives touched
How many faces brightened.

Whatever the greatness of Justiceville
    the comrade is at the heart
Whatever spirit reigns in Justiceville
    the comrade is the spark.

Enjoy life now, comrade
Do not forget us
But do not look back
Live life, comrade
And grab God's great bounty!

You and Me

Define yourself
As I define myself
What you think of me
Store in the vaults
Of the unknown
Until you are ready
To declare yourself.

Find your own way
As I have mine
Be secure
Discern your strength
Assert your right
To the sun
Compassion will reach
The grateful
Bear witness to
The empowerment of all
The potency of joy.

I snub not the world
I invite the world to accept me
Like minds
And concerted actions
Inaugurating a time of change.

Trump what the world thinks of you
With what you think of the world
Supply content
To the bravado
So that it matters
In a cycle of rebirth.

Rhythms of Hope

The perfect day has arrived
A day without sins
No more a time of preparation.
Self review
Ceaseless woes
Ceaseless wonder
All abandoned
In the rubble heap.
The soul is
As always before
Toned and ready.

Humility flows
A life-giving breath
    Frenetic thoughts silenced
    Doubts forgotten
    Dull urges faded
    Truthful desires balanced
The heart pumps the blood
Of the treasures of earth and heaven.
The moment
Potent and open
Provides direction
New habits find room to grow
Performing, fulfilling, discharging –
Satisfied completion in the everyday.

Ask the past and present:
    What is the historiography of hope?
    Can we discern its every instance?
    Honor its inhalation and exhalation?
    Discover our traditions of movement?

Enflesh
These abstract questions
These moral imperatives
In our everyday
Make real our every breath
The engine of our agency
The impatience of patience
The patience of impatience
Open horizons
Meeting, listening
Clear rhythms, strong energies
Conscious breath made life.

Reinventing Tradition

The grandiose self
Kept an eye on
A resplendent future
A frozen gaze
From the guarded present.

The people's unextinguished faith
In the promises of a benevolent state
The conduit
For a comforting globalism.
Tradition remains elsewhere
Offering peace
A source of stability
Spirits to be re-embodied
Whatever the twists and turns
Wrought by history's ruptures.

An established force
An emerging power
Accumulated wisdom
Beyond constraints
The ground for living
Creativity and struggle
Regenerating relations
With depth
Integrity
And futurity.

Violate the perfect stasis
Of an idealized future
Serving as a blind spot
A closing off
Instead of an enabling hope.

Futurity

Gamble with time
To win the future
Already part of the present
To intensify presence
The basis of hope
Sufficient to transform
The experience of the moment
The basis of action

Dream of today
Forget the trials
Ignore the omens
Grab the whirlwind
Blowing fulfillment your way

Repair the heart
Stop its bleeding
Insert courage
Warm the mind
Smile!
Clear the throat
Utter the words
About days ahead
When the pains are gone
With new rains
To fertilize the land

Hope for Wholeness

I know no one anymore
Voices buried
In lands that know no one
Rejection is the rule
Purging all of afflictions.

A new future
Politicized domains
Contested options
Confused minds:
    accept the new
    reject the old
    purge the body
    displace the legs
New inventions
Clever struggles
As history is transcended.

I recall tradition
Reclaim meanings
To regenerate resistance
Renewing minds
And forging new bodies.

Redemption

Grinned teeth in the theater of absurdity
Like eyes, watching the end of history
The aroma of chaos
Dropping saliva from mouths ajar
Opened to utter curses.

Pronounce the causes
Utter no curses
The fragrance of seduction
Flavors the moment's troubles
The quarrel between home and world
Compels identification
Disorienting self and action.

Revitalize history
Invent traditions
Engage the surroundings
The abode of culture
In cults of friendship.

Rites of passage reborn
To confront consequence
Engineer mentorship
Recarve horizons
Excite desire
To imagine
The paths of fulfillment.

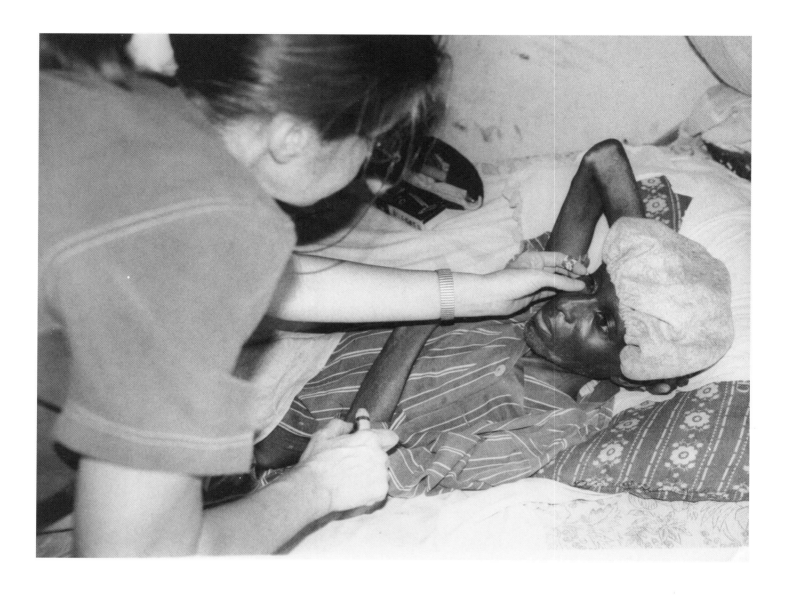

Wellness

One day's fever
Kills the health
Of twelve months
Illness enters the body
Without warning
With less difficulty
Than when
It departs.

Illness that gives notice
Does not kill the patient
When sickness rides a horse
The sick board the jet
"Conceal me and I cause you death"
Is the name of sickness
Accept the fragility
Of living
Apologize to Misfortune
Offer sacrifices
To placate the anger
Of the harbinger of Death.

If you lack time to attend your illness
You have time to die
The bold does not conceal illness
The bold has time
Seek forgiveness
Repay the iniquities
To reverse the evils.

We worship you
The frail and fragile
We respect you
The erring human
Sick people are like kings
Today we regard you as a king
    Your majesty
    Lord of illness
    Master of death
For staying alive.

Tragic to Yogic Life

Death has deprived me of my mother
My father, devoured by death
My life
An interlude
Awaiting death

Cast your glance at me
A few more days
Drain this life of emptiness

I am unconscious
I invite death
Subconscious of blunders
Yearnings planted in an arid land
of desolate sounds

My breath deepens
A fecund stillness
Descending its claim to the earth
Rejuvenated veins
Quiet work, announce not
every step
Undiscover the impulse
to record every reflection
The intricacy of death

My riches of emptiness
Vital voices
coursing through my frame
Loving awareness
bestowing peace
Resolute rejoicing
nourishing wonder
As always and after
the rekindled
yogic life

Anger

Red colors
The fabric of Self
The red black blood
Pulsing through clenched eyes
A throbbing universe of wrath
Spaces of conflict
Soaked in tension
To negotiate
Inequality
And exclusion

Boast in caution
Tuck yesterday's emotion away
To fulfill today's mission
Forgetting
Forgiving
To make a pleasant day

Humility

Teach me to be humble.
Do I think too much of myself,
or not enough of others?
I saw what many couldn't see,
and sometimes yelled my truth.
I rejected platitudes and convention,
unconvinced and uncompelled.
I defied the rewards of conformity,
the belonging bestowed
by meeting expectations.
If some challenges for me were easy,
I didn't humiliate those who struggled.

Cut down your size, but
keep your wardrobe.
The mouth remains shut, to
let the ears listen.
Humility trusts the unknown,
opens to the gods,
discerns the genius of others, and
welcomes the wondrous future.

If I didn't reject praise, I was not immodest.
If I sought affirmation, I was not selfish.
Leadership found me, and
my purpose was to serve.
We are fighting formidable enemies
in the midst of the indifferent,
and those who have never
glimpsed the responsibilities of hope.
My large claims, my grandiosity
were only to engineer ruptures, create alternatives.
Must we not be humble with the humble,
arrogant with the arrogant?

Slavery, servitude and humility
are sisters
in the eyes of the arrogant.
You may be a warrior.
Yours may be to chart new territory.
But grandiosity of intention rots,
deceives itself and becomes pathetic,
consumes itself with doubt and loneliness,
and dishonors the fight.
Grandiosity is the prerogative of youth;
in sprouting elders, a violence.
Humility seems a luxury
to the blind warrior,
a counter-intuitive tongue
unable to speak the real story.

I have come to the limits of myself.
Words I could spin; the arguments
I brandished led to nowhere.
Why didn't the world change?
Recognizing that I am small
before the grandness of
God, the collective grandness of others,
that achievements cannot
be credited to the self alone,
I relinquish my bold claims.
How am I different from others?
Come, let us join hands.

Humility and passivity
are enemies.
Humility and openness
great friends.
Test openness,
a difficult exam to pass.
Neither blind acceptance
nor apologetic resignation.
Useless as general principle,
make sympathy specific.
Enter anger and then
restrain the self; listen
to close the distance
and cement trust with gratitude.

Humility is not the opposite of arrogance,
Humility is the opposite of despair,
born of disconnection, marred
by addiction—Yes, I know all this,
but the glimpses refuse to ignite.
My ego—vessel and demon.
My obligations abdicated,
I do not act.

No longer a time for the big:
no big solutions, no final
answers to desire and recognition.
Change through the small, the
daily efforts of duty.
Quiet gestures on a new path,
leaving the worn grooves
of ease and destruction.
Fathom anew
Nourish identity
Sympathize with your faltering—
Steady paces to a worthy end.

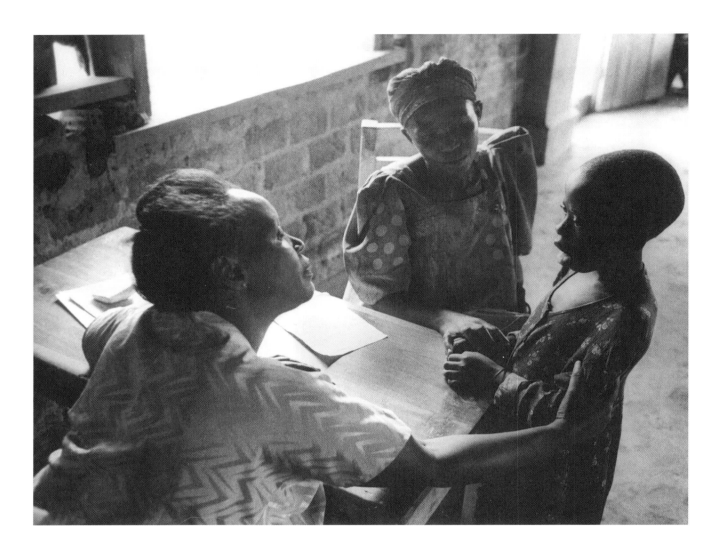

Giving

The train marches on!
Taking us to a destination
Of hope
We are the marching train
As many
Bonded by our gifts
Of giving.

People!
Shall we
        give without expectation
        receive without reward
Gestures and tokens
Laughter and enthusiasm
Uplifting the minds
Easing hearts
Seeking the contentment
Of our spirits expressed?

Yet giving
Can house a will to power
Making blind
To giving's humble magic.
And forgetting oneself
In the imperative to give
Distorts and deludes.
Give not to repress the self.

Exchanges of peace
Terminating despair
Healing wounds
Bringing bliss
Watering the lawns of life.

Serving

Evacuate the cave of despair
The mixture of mates
Shattering doubts
Repudiating nihilism
Cleansing pains.

Serve, without power
Affirm, without surprises
Trust, without paralysis
Choose duty, without rewards
May the self expand
To make selfishness bountiful.

Serve in peace
To promote peace
Agitation of the mind
    not of war
Confusion of methods
    not of conflicts
Hunger in the belly
    not of poverty
Headaches and colds
    not the spread of AIDS.

Collaborate and connect
With one and many
Give and receive
    to confer power
    to reinvent tradition
Listen, be present
    to dignify sympathy
    to enhance relations
    to promote the whole
    to create harmony
An embrace of
Sacrifice
To make Holy.

Leadership

Lead with humility
Leadership is no birthright
Only an opportunity to serve
Joining others
To define themselves
To develop oneself.

Know thyself
Affirm history
Reclaim desire
Discover the visceral power
Of engagement
Seek the materiality
And evanescence
Of relationships
Cherish individuality
Welcome the initiatives of others
Communal moments
Discover deep structures
Of culture and earth
As routine
As ritual
Enabling structures
That require faith.

Embody generosity
Leadership in hospitality
Self-assertion in creativity
In spaces of encounter
Receive the hospitality of others
An investment
in pluri-cultural space.

A serpent's heart is small
Leader, do not become one
A small mouth can open wide
Enough to spit venom
Make the mouth sensitive
Humanize the tongue
To talk to the deaf
Make the lame walk
Fill hungry stomachs.

The bee does not trouble the lion
The elephant is not afraid of the ant
Free the mind
To walk freely
The lion cannot eat the bee
Ant is no food for the elephant
Do not become the hyena
Eating goat for supper
Eat goodness
Humility for breakfast
Service for lunch
Affection for dinner
To digest dignity.

Authority

A moral horizon
A set of edicts
The representation of force
Beyond the coercive and the persuasive
The alchemy of duty and action.

Tame yourself
Stabilize your household
Measure achievements to offer calm
Endure insults
Acquire persistence
And cultivate patience.

Intervene
Urgently
Intensely
To convene
Encounters of dialogue
Theaters of transformation.

Refuse the hammer that
    imposes answers
    compels listening
    demands obedience
Fire does not quench fire.

Chemistry of emotions
Kairos of authority
Divining when the other
May be changed
Instantaneously
In the heat of
Generosity and purpose.

Souls Unchained

I proclaim:
Reject all burdens,
all obligations
Resist the pressure
to conform, to respond
Refuse the weighty tasks
of the other's happiness.

I teach:
Give yourself the benefit
of your self-doubt
Retain your fears
Reclaim your anxieties
Confront solemn questions
on your honorable journey.

You wonder:
Why me?
Why court me, woo me?
Stalk me with poetry?
Why offer me such ardent gifts?
Why reveal such intense talents?
Am I goddess to his supplication?

I answer:
No outcomes sought
No repayment
of gesture for gesture,
logic for logic
An intuition has been ignited
What he wants
you have already:
    self-knowledge
    self-love
    divinity
    your excited heart
Bask in the glory of his attention
You owe him nothing.

I invite:
See more of him
Beyond talent and charm
The powerful self
and its sources:
    forceful and righteous
    compassionate and tender
    arrogant and grandiose
    fearful and self-doubting
    presumptuous and patronizing
    humble and grateful
    contemptuous and harsh
    delighted and engaged.

I urge:
Show yourself:
    your deepest creativity
    fierce and gentle yearnings
    aspirations and fears
    broken resolutions
    despairing frustrations
    wisdom and foolishness
    selfishness and generosity
    reverence and hunger.

I conclude:
Prepare yourself
for momentous decisions
Seize the ammunition
to fight the wars of emotions
with those who disregard lessons
at inopportune times.

Two Become One

Lovely and sacred
To embrace the
Quiet wonder
And open possibility
Of the everyday,
Shared in the warmth
And trusting comfort
Of another.
May your future hold
Such everydays,
Moments so simple,
Regular as breath
Taken in
Released.

Magic marriage box –
Never too empty
Never too full,
Filled with gifts
Found treasures
Collected beauty.
When the box
Discovers the alchemy
Of your love and faith,
When its happy fullness
Must burst,
Your gifts and treasures
Venture forth to
Deliver honor and joy.

Your blessed marriage
Your cherished home
A haven to lend strength
To inspire peace
For you, for others.
An untold mystery:
Into the private home
Of man and wife
The whole world flows.

40 Years and 40 Days

Can we count 41 years?
A shared journey
The distance traveled
Over a lifetime together.

Time, distance, arrival
Immeasurable by standard terms:
Achievements, wealth,
Success of children.

Is it 41 years?
The passage of time is swift
Unfolding destinies
Unmasking possibilities.

It is 41 years!
Astrologers count numbers
41 can mean something planetic
Half a century is close.

40 years and 40 days!
Thrilling passage of time
Solemnity encoded
Surprises discovered.

40 days and 40 years
Enough to make histories
The unfolding of truths
The death of pain.

It is 41 years!
Yet another 40 await
Rich histories made for
The hungry grasp of the future.

Rich histories
Future's Past
Histories our foundation
The ground upon which we walk.

Cherish memory
Keep history
All its hopes and lessons
Lessons of hope.

Treasures of memory
Some we cannot keep
We cannot count, we cannot inventory
All the baubles, all the riches.

40 years minus 5
Five years of ignorance
Ignorance is no shame
Memory can recover.

The rest is clear
Like light through glass
More visible than darkness
White as snow.

Let me now talk more
Revealing portions of love
Slices of a mango
To devour and savor.

A hidden album with
Pictures past
Never before revealed
Dust covering histories.

Clean the dust
Reveal the ultimate truth
Dignity remembered
As the sun finds its place.

Treasured faces
Memories of freshness
Youthful minds
Looking onto an unknown.

The unknown of promise
A future far but near
Measure the journey of faces
From past to present.

Bonded travels, shared agonies
Occasions for staging and fulfilling
The great questions and challenges
That define us.

[continued]

Our independent selves
Our fierce convictions
Unquenchable vitality
Distinct visions of peace and wholeness.

Yes, these too are
Locked with the other
In countless acts of care
The gift of our own otherness.

Half a century to come
Awaiting the daily chores
And extravagant visions
To intersect the spirits.

The final truth is here
40 years and 40 days filled with
Dignity and integrity
Paving our way.

Familiar Family

Hate lies
Saying that love is a lie
Sorrow lies
Saying that friendship rots
But here love precedes hate
To show us a truth
Bigger than good
The journey begun with kindness
For sorrow to escape.

Landmarks of the familiar
Living in steady minds
Stamped by
The family of reunions
Unions of hospitality
The joining of success
The sharing of sorrows.

No one is invisible
Even when misunderstood
Horizons projected by
History and authority
Where desire and ambition
Are insufficient to destroy
Collective capacities.

Wrinkles of experience
Moonlight stories of
Communal feasts
The labors of home
Reaching beyond the family
Celebrations with
Affectionate ostentation
The overflow of emotion
Rites of passage
Self-regulation
Calm and peace.

Grey hairs of wisdom
Prove the well-being
Of our family
Our wealth of virtues:
    generosity
    respect for elders
    commemorating our dead
Pleasures and emotions
Cohabitate with
Duty and prosperity.

Mama

A life without rest
The restlessness of work
Feeding the babies
Nursing the adults
Managing wallets
Resolving conflicts
The spoon wielder
    controlling the pots
The prolific banana tree
    bearing limitless fruit.

Beacon of calmness
Ever smiling
To hide the pain
Caused by others
The pain of fear
Of an unknown future.

Mama, the Queen
Wisdom of the home
Like whiteness
    the beauty of the teeth
Like erectness
    the glory of the neck
Mama is the King.

The chameleon
Smiling when others smile
Crying to challenge cries
Singing to add to songs
Laughing to compound joy
Wrestling in storms
Playful, the toy of others
Bank of wisdom
Keeper of secrets
Whispered secrets
Shielded by the heart
That sees the future
The destination
Of success and rebirth.

Mama, I bow my head to the ground
    to become a spirit
Mama, I bow to you
    to become immortal
Mama, I bow to thee
Put the crown on my head
To sit on the throne of awe.

Sister's Band

An annual band
From sister to brother
A bracelet of love
That I have worn
Until threadbare
Two hearts melded
Turning into steel

My sister
Come with me
Distance is not so sweet
To lure you from me
Sister, leave the face of fright
The sickening scourge
That Mama dreads
The frenzy, fatal to
Papa's health

Sister, abandon
The serial killer of hope
That plagues our home
Blights our verandah
Perverting our humanity
Raping our sanity

Sister, come to me
Forget the chaos
That destroys our minds
Abandon the perils
The stench of hate
Come to me
See your band that I wear
To awaken the family souls
To plant new seeds
Tomorrow's flowers
New scents
In a beautiful land

Comfort Zone

I leave the Ivory Tower
To return no more
The drought that famished me
I head to the abandoned family
To see the bare feet
Stepping on the sands of contentment.

A renewed plunge
Into the pool of humanity
Bidding farewell to harvests of sadness
Renewed energies unpacked
From the luggage of drought.

Bountiful gifts
Shared with a collective heart
Instinctive hospitality
Exchanged with appreciation
Love and care
The desire to know me
To see me succeed and prosper
As I leave pains behind.

The gift of food
Stored in stomachs without aches
Living legends
Taking questions
Horizons of new representation
Trusting the integrity of place
Citations forgotten
Footnotes erased
As I receive
    without asking
    without knowing
    that I had need
The force of giving
An otherness
To make me whole.

Rains drop
The clouds clear
I see a new sky
Revealing another world
Of duty unencumbered.

A widening circle
Welcoming vistas of emotion
Natural and free
Exposing the tragedy of dislocation
And now again
An awakening
Sufficient to ennoble me.

Hospitality

Ocean of love and labor
More than brick and mortar
Abode of peace and harmony
Shelter of the sacred
The site of love's labor
Countless contributions
At a varied pace
To fulfill all
A space that nurtures
A place of growth
Offering relief and renewal
Attracting respect and honor.

Our hospitable home
A joint venture
Untainted by infidelity
Without diminishment
What a treasure and luxury
An honor and duty
To be possessed
By such a home
Welcoming others
Inviting their faith
Effortless gestures
Mutual gratitude
Communal responsibility
Weaving the fabric of life
Without expectation.

Serve the food
Quench the thirst
May the laughter soar
　　the music give your feet flight
　　soft words comfort your sorrow
　　the blankets cover you well
Our home is your home.

Homecoming

I come to touch the soil
Land of my birth
I am here to feel
Warmth and affection
I want to see
All that is glorious
Give me
News of celebrations

I travel alone
Wife, I have none
Look at me
All sides
Spread the perfume
Perform the contacts
To let me travel back
As a twin

I am not part of them
The errand boy
Of those who kill
And trample on the dead
I leave their woes behind:
     futility of politics
     arrogance of power
     subjugation of others

Exclude me from it
It of power
It of disease
It of hunger
It of genocide
It of oppression

Include me in it
It of love
It of affection
It of charity
It of compassion
It of security

The pilgrim has wheels
Rolling towards the street of
     Joy
Through the alleys of
     Happiness
Passing through the cove of
     Memory
To the cul-de-sac of
     History

The Wedding Guest

The wedding season is upon us
Bringing bushels of joy
Our darling young people
To be sent to new worlds of
Marital adventure
Creating new realities
New streams of the future
What glorious blessings!
But beware, for danger lurks.

Times of feasting and
Opulent banquets
The tandoor oven fired
Samosas and kebabs mountained high
Curries glistening with
Spicy temptation
A gushing river of mango lassi
Gulab jamuns impatient,
Awaiting their turn at the
Mouth's guillotine
Only a rumali roti could
Wipe the tears of joy!
But beware, for danger lurks.

Deliriously delicious events but even
Gargantuan buffets can be exhausted
O, beware the notorious guest!
His voraciousness competing only
With his unabashedness
Devouring everything in sight
Pleading his case in various guises
Attempting to win your indulgence.
Don't be alarmed
Prepare for all eventualities
Forewarned is forearmed!

1) The Misleadingly Modest
"Is it every day or even every
year that I arrive at your
doorstep? Is it too much
to feed me a small morsel if
I am hungry? Can you not
spare a tiny thimble of cold
water if I am parched? Is there
not a small corner where I
can rest my weary feet without
giving too much trouble?"

2) The Foreign Dignitary
"Do you know the distance I have
traveled? I represent a great
empire, so you should regard my
very presence as a gift of freedom and
democracy (and the liberation of your
women, time permitting). Look,
either provide suitable hospitality
or I will send U.N. inspectors to hunt for
utensils of mass consumption."

3) The Exceptionally Vain
"Is it not a great delight and
gift for your other guests simply
to look upon me, to enjoy my
company? Listen, I understand
we are here to honor the bride
and groom, but you must admit I am
very charming and handsome. By
the way, I don't believe you will
strain your arm by bringing
me some more puris and sabzi."

Watch for these scenarios
Seemingly innocent or abruptly aggressive
Your gentle natures unprepared
To provide any defense against
Such subtle or direct assaults.

National Crisis: Food Shortage!
Such guests, at the very least, should
Give advance notice of
The impending catastrophe.
The Government may be put on alert
Relief agencies contacted
Grassroots mobilizations supplementing
        the deficit.
The citizenry can sacrifice in the
        national interest
Eating less to satiate the gluttonous guest.

Worry not, good friends
Can you pick and choose your guests?
Your fear and caution are unfounded
My appetite will bring you honor
I will anoint the bride and groom
Celebrate me as I celebrate you!

The Spirituality of Politics

You worship a particular god
Why not be this or that god?
Join the traffic
Between heaven and earth
Faith is also our oxygen
The faithful
Enduring violence
Destined to taste destruction
Faith remains
Thread in the
Fabric of movement.

When wrath is virtuous
Individual propensities
Unique proclivities
Purposeful efforts
Yield the potent freedom
Of the answering self.

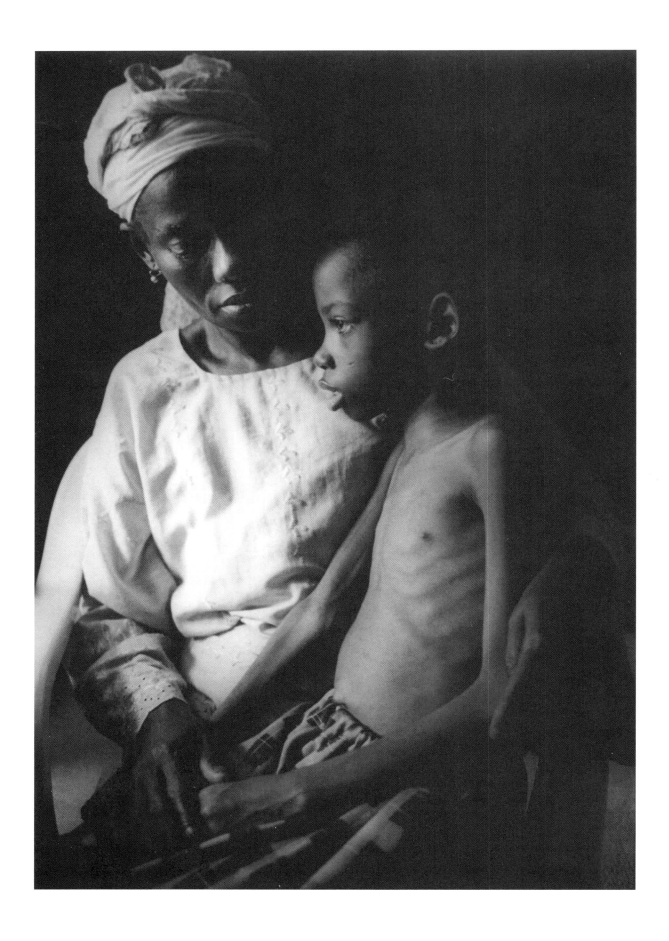

Desert Love

Today is the day to celebrate
Celebrate with joy and peace
Contemplate the grand
Growth of yesteryear
Unmeasured success.

Next year is on its way
Traveling, walking, moving
Not another January 1st
Of broken resolutions.

Transform the internal soul
Renovate the external self
The front facing the world's turmoil
The back to be stabbed by world hunger
Two sides surrounded by AIDS.

Where is our savior?
If Jesus Christ is yet to revisit
A thankful reflection
The goodness of humankind
In the image of God
Our deficiencies will be too clear.

Our savior is here
Recollecting the uncertainty
Of our long possession
To make us grateful
To inspire humility
To teach us moderation
To proclaim we are loved.

Diaspora's Task

The language of passion
Of creativity unbound
The skill to uproot evil
The talent to rethink
Newness.

Modernity is no stranger
Its sources not despised
As nationalism unfolds
Even the conqueror may be
Reconfigured to fuel
Our vital power once again.

Fresh talents
Uncharted paths
The privileges and duties
Of our universalism
Our humanism
Nourish our poor
Repackage our culture
To give us breath.

Power's seduction
Potent processes
Reimage achievement
Reconstruct efficiency
To cleanse the mind
Purify the body
And liberate the soul.

The flag of productivity unfurls
What wind can shake it?
A flag mightier than the wind.

The Spirit of Ancestors

Spirit, carried by the gods
Or are the gods dead?
Nay, not the ancestors
Our dead do not die
Awaken our champions to
Cure our deafness

Elders, officers of golden fire
Keepers of the gate
Know our dreams and hopes
Feel our fears and triumphs
Release us, those who have come before
Free us, those who come after

Assassins and abdicators!
Chores of spirit neglected
Find the truants, lash the guilty
I need, we need
Joy Wisdom Peace
Carry our hope against forgetting

The man wears the mask
Lost and seeking
Afraid of shadows
Seeking counsel, seeking rebirth
Insolent and impatient
Ungrateful and brave

Elders are also human
Busy or perplexed
Resources exhausted
Blame them not
Laughing then, crying now
Tasks multiplied in talk too dense

Elders old, elders new
The dead talk and talk
Answer them not
The dead do not disappear
Dreams raise their heads
To commune and transform

Assembly of gods
Elders in attendance
Free counsel with the dead
Wisdom woven
Patience unignored
See, touch, feel

Sunlight and rains
Wash us fresh and alive
Thunder and dust
Shock us solemn and alert
Earth and black
Restore us with rest and dream

Zapatista Salute

The dust from the distance rises
To cover the cloud
The harmattan of change
The hurricane of a new order.

New imperial wars
Boundless cynicism
Villainy of neoliberalism
Tigritude of World Bankism
Flowing like the River Blood
Water that is our new poison.

Terminate oppression
Kill hunger
Pour the rain of mercy
Protests, agitations
Mobilizing, strategizing
We are not unmindful fools
We are the people insurgent
Marching from our Cave of Hope.

Commandos, rise up!
Remove not thy masks
Until tomorrow comes
Thy tasks remain
Uncompleted work
For legs in the midst of thorns
Bold agendas
Of dignity and justice.

Come, come, come
Reclaim the commons
Invent democratic spaces
Discover horizontal leadership
Discharge obligations.

Come, come, come
Convene the encounter of many worlds
Share the collective word
Let our history walk again
To inaugurate People's Power.

Commanders, we salute
We trust you
In ourselves
Our tasks conjoined
To produce another day
A day that was not yesterday.

Another task
The task of Peace
Our formidable ventures conjoined
We are not heartless interlocutors
Fake peacemakers
Destroying fragile gains
Commanders, we salute.

Transnationalism

From Africa dispersed
With hearts open to learn
With minds and hands ready to work,
We journeyed to escape constriction
To make our mark
To give our children opportunities
To build the world anew.
Our motherland is not forgotten –
She is who we are
She carries our heart
We carry her spirit
We hear her calls
Our lives and efforts answer her.

We have arrived
In this haughty land of hate and money
With its unrivalled genius for theft
With creative talent for misrepresentation
With unapologetic achievements of ignorance
With maudlin gestures of self-congratulation
With unending words of justification
Debating the pros and cons of slavery
Draining our treasures
Relishing and pitying our death
Seeing Africa as beggar
Launching wars with dishonorable swords
Bloodletting to cure the world of Blackness.

Our hopes have turned to lament
Our hunger for justice mocked
Our thirst for respect ridiculed
Our quest for a future crushed.
Are we helpless observers
Or guilty participants?
Is our outrage pointless,
The laughable cry of the vanquished?

Wait! The marathon has not yet ended.
Our migrating voices carve the path ahead.
Our tongues lead the way
In a race we all can win,
Even carrying the tortoise on our backs.
Our tigers roar with fiery eyes
Our wisdom calms with understanding
Our plaintive howls can be soothed
Our songs of hope soar again.

We race!
We stride together
Our muscles strengthen with each day
We walk, we run
We breathe, we drink
We rest, we eat
We race into our future of dignity.

We salute our voices!
Resolute and fierce
Judicious and restrained
Generous and visionary
Champions of love and pride.
When giants stride
The earth must tremble.

The Oxygen of Culture

Feast upon our ordinary lives
Drink our hearts and devour our flesh
Receive the fire of our young
The sacred eyes of our poor
We who are weak and strong
We who are edge and center
Become the traffic between us
Empty yourself so we may labor within you.

Learn our wordless language
Decipher its grammar and meaning
Expand its lexicon and force
Beckon to yourself
  our genius and ecstasy
  our confusion and cruelty
  our failures and faith
Beautify our hapless chaos
Assemble the threads
For a fabric to shelter us and unveil our spirit.
Our forgotten dreams
And ten thousand truths
Will flood forth from your mouth.

Breathe deeply of us
  the determined dust of duty
  the swirling fumes of grief
  the honeyed morning of hope
  the ominous frost of rage
  the dank stench of despair
  the wooded night sky of passion
Your lungs must become vast,
Your heart commanding.
Those who have come before
Will walk with us through you.

You are our pride and conviction
Let us hold you
Until you rise to hold us
Lose yourself in us
As we await our discovery.
You must not forget us,
Trapped in your inner designs.
Be gentle when we do not see truth
Forgive us if we fail
Your heart and its longings.
Only you can understand
Your questions and your magic.
Undertake the journey to trust yourself
Invent the rituals to fulfill your purpose:
Radiant compassion scripted
In a body of supple strength.

Another Gathering

Brothers and sisters, no one need inform us
that we suffer, enlighten us that there is
injustice, placate us with practical piths
of patience. Throughout our enduring
agonies, we have responded, we have
fought. We have drawn from our genius
to survive. We have learned from each
other and from our history. In spite of
our courage, our creativity, our love, and
our efforts, we have sometimes been defeated,
our talents exhausted, our maneuvers of
hope and regeneration trumped by evil
shadows ever ready to devour us. Yet even in
our anguished exhaustion, our overflowing
perplexity, our faith has never been
extinguished, the blood strength of our soul.
Our faith will take us beyond what we
have known, what we have tried. Today, our
faith has brought us to seek each other
anew. What secrets do we bear, unbeknownst
to us, that can mingle to unravel our woes?

We must revisit old questions. Who or what
excludes us? Which forces in their haughty
majesty subordinate us? How do mysterious
abstractions and the false logic of money enslave
us? What decaying social structures burden
us with miserly alibi? How does culture
at once give us life and stifle our breath?
How did we arrive here, and what can be
done? Sisters and brothers, these are difficult,
urgent questions, but they are not new.
Our lives have attempted answers with
dignity and commitment. We have wanted
new paths for our children. We have prayed:
Let them know the best of us and carry forth
the gifts of grace we have received. But let them
not suffer as we have suffered. Let them create
a world with fresh tools that do not bear
the shame of our failures, the rust of our despair.

[continued]

Today is new only in that we are gambling
one day's time that there is something yet
that our everyday lives and struggles have
not unlocked. That in posing the questions
together, in nurturing the politics of listening,
some new insight, however small, may
ignite us, teach us that our talent is
boundless, that we walk forward into
history, that we are not doomed to repeat
the piteous dance of suffering and earnest
failure, draining our last strength and resolve.
Brothers and sisters, look upon our charmed
chamber. Today, it keeps the pernicious
forces at bay, for our time of reflection
and learning, for the mystical engineering
of hope and genius. There is no pomp
and circumstance here, but our space
of meeting has been beautified, food
and water plentiful for the day. The magic time
of our labor of sacred listening, the blessed
time of knowing ourselves again for the daily
work of duty and care and joy. We dare
to hope that a maze need not be a dungeon.

Sisters and brothers, we all know each other,
some better than others. Some we may never
know, no matter how much we talk. We may not
like everyone equally, or at all. Today, may our
prejudices, even the justified ones, temporarily
evaporate. Our collective gifts have allowed
us to survive violence, the injustices imposed
from without and within, the squandering
of our young, the ignominy endured by our elders.
Some of us have known how to fight; we will
listen to them and learn. Some of us have known
how to carry on; from them too we will learn.
Some have not known how to fight or to carry on,
but we are here together, and they will also teach us.
Some have helped us forget our sorrows long enough
to laugh; we cannot live without them. In this,
the space of our shared work, let us call forth
and bear witness to the smallest feelings and
thoughts and instincts that can guide us. What
we believed we knew will be surprised and
augmented today. Even if we forget and

return to our convictions about ourselves and
others, our large-hearted inquiries will bear fruit.

Brothers and sisters, I have spoken to you
of our hopes, our hearts full of good purpose
this early morning. But this day will be
long; the conversations may become tedious
and repetitive; you may become bored and
tired. Several among us have prepared
for today's undertaking. A few will attempt
to ensure that all voices may be heard,
to keep our energies focused, but they are not
experts. They are still learning, and may be
shy or nervous. We can find within ourselves
the capacity to learn from those who are also
trying to learn, to remain aware of our purpose,
to allow hope to clothe us with sweet shelter.
We may falter today. Why should we not?
In today's modest gesture of our self-love,
can the missteps be so momentous, so
disastrous? Let us resolve to trust one another.

Sisters and brothers, we can glimpse our horizon
but not insist on its meaning. Our exertions
today feed our horizon. Today, let us not ask
our horizon to feed us. Let us resist
the fanaticism that can lie in our own hearts.
Today is a reminder of our strength, an invitation
to renew it, multiply it. Even as we prepare
for battle, our goal is not to crush the enemy,
but to protect the conditions for our dignity.
Let us refuse the violence of purifying ourselves
in the name of fighting oppression. It is enough
that today we experience and feel that our
listening and speaking, sharing our questions
and answers, transform us and give us new maps.
Still, by today's end, we will not all be on the
same page. Knowledge is not homogeneous.
Some among us will be impatient. They may see,
or think they see, more clearly than the rest.
Their work on our behalf will be tireless,
may make disconcerting demands. Let us honor
their impatience and zeal. Others of us may be slow,
meditative, seemingly content with meditation.
Let us honor their patience or indecision.

[continued]

207

Beautiful ones, my people, no matter the magic of today, whether dull or glistening, tomorrow's old work will still await us. Our work today, even if it soon fades in our memory, will enliven us, enrich us, strengthen us, and reunite learning with hope and action. And tonight's dance and song will radiate with our reawakening spirit. The freedom of assembly is nothing less than the freedom of alchemy.

List of Photographs